"Who I truly am—what Gregory Gans[illegible] my core identity—is a function of who and what I love the most. In this engaging and accessible book, Ganssle offers a compelling account of our deepest desires—the ones we cannot escape and would not if we could. Ganssle finds in the wisdom of the Christian tradition compelling support for his vision of how to get and stay on the right track in life. Believers and nonbelievers alike have much to gain from his warm and wise engagement with the question. Only a great teacher could have written a book like this."

Anthony Kronman, Sterling Professor of Law, Yale University

"*Our Deepest Desires* is a little gem of a book, written with the clarity and wisdom of a seasoned teacher. Learned yet accessible, Ganssle takes his readers on a fresh tour of life's big questions by tracking ways the claims of Christianity connect up with fundamental human longings. This may be our new *Mere Christianity*, and it will surely inspire conversations worth having."

Eric Gregory, professor of religion and chair of the council of the humanities, Princeton University

"Christian philosophers and apologists have spilled much ink defending the truth of Christianity—rightly so, given the rise of New Atheism and other movements that call into question Christianity's plausibility. What has been widely neglected, however, is showing the desirability of Jesus and the gospel. In this brilliantly written book, Gregory Ganssle shows how the Christian story makes sense of our deepest longings—for love, beauty, truth, goodness, and freedom. I highly recommend this book to anyone who is interested in finding a story that is both true to the way things are and true to the way things ought to be."

Paul M. Gould, assistant professor of philosophy and Christian apologetics, Southwestern Baptist Theological Seminary, Fort Worth, Texas

"We live in a time in the West when Christianity is implausible to many because it doesn't seem to be good. While frequently and unwittingly still assuming intuitions that echo our Christian past, late moderns have ironically come to see Christianity as a threat to human flourishing. Nonbelievers don't just think Christianity is wrong, they find it distasteful. This calls for an apologetic that appeals not only to the head but also to the heart. The need is to help unbelievers see that Christianity is not only true, it is beautiful. This is where Gregory Ganssle's book comes in—drawing on rich Christian resources of the past and winsomely dialoguing with competing secular stories. With both clarity and grace, *Our Deepest Desires* points to how the Christian story offers more explanatory power than its chief rivals."

Joshua D. Chatraw, executive director, Center for Apologetics and Cultural Engagement, Liberty University

OUR DEEPEST DESIRES

How the Christian Story Fulfills Human Aspirations

GREGORY E. GANSSLE

An imprint of InterVarsity Press
Downers Grove, Illinois

InterVarsity Press
P.O. Box 1400, Downers Grove, IL 60515-1426
ivpress.com
email@ivpress.com

InterVarsity Press® is the book-publishing division of InterVarsity Christian Fellowship/USA®, a movement of students and faculty active on campus at hundreds of universities, colleges, and schools of nursing in the United States of America, and a member movement of the International Fellowship of Evangelical Students. For information about local and regional activities, visit intervarsity.org.

While any stories in this book are true, some names and identifying information may have been changed to protect the privacy of individuals.

Cover design: Cindy Kiple
Interior design: Daniel van Loon
Images: © Petorn/iStockphoto

ISBN 978-0-8308-5182-9 (print)
ISBN 978-0-8308-9095-8 (digital)

Printed in the United States of America ♾

As a member of the Green Press Initiative, InterVarsity Press is committed to protecting the environment and to the responsible use of natural resources. To learn more, visit greenpressinitiative.org.

Library of Congress Cataloging-in-Publication Data
Names: Ganssle, Gregory E., 1956- author.
Title: Our deepest desires : how the Christian story fulfills human aspirations / Gregory E. Ganssle.
Description: Downers Grove : InterVarsity Press, 2017. | Includes index.
Identifiers: LCCN 2017022344 (print) | LCCN 2017019248 (ebook) | ISBN 9780830890958 (eBook) | ISBN 9780830851829 (pbk. : alk. paper)
Subjects: LCSH: Jesus Christ--Person and offices. | Christianity--Essence, genius, nature. | Desire--Religious aspects--Christianity.
Classification: LCC BT203 (print) | LCC BT203 .G363 2017 (ebook) | DDC 233--dc23
LC record available at https://lccn.loc.gov/2017022344

P 25 24 23 22 21 20 19 18 17 16 15 14 13 12 11 10 9 8 7 6 5 4 3 2 1
Y 37 36 35 34 33 32 31 30 29 28 27 26 25 24 23 22 21 20 19 18 17

For some lifelong friends

David Horner

David Kanne

Kurt Richardson

With lifelong gratitude.

CONTENTS

Acknowledgments

These thoughts have been simmering for several years. As a result, I have many people to thank for help and encouragement along the way. My first attempt to speak on these matters was due to an invitation by the Yale Christian Fellowship. I want to thank Greg Hendrickson for the invitation and the Yale Secular Student Alliance, who participated with a rigorous discussion. That talk was later published in *Logos: Yale's Journal of Christian Thought*. Annie Vo was then editor and did much to help me clarify my work. An early version of about half of this book was discussed over several weeks by Craig Leukens and Dashell Laryea. I appreciate their insightful comments. My son Nick also read chunks and offered his writer's touch.

I presented versions of this work at Vienna Presbyterian Church, the Mount Airy Apologetics Conference, St. John's Episcopal Church, the University of Massachusetts, the University of Missouri, and the University of New Hampshire as well as at a joint meeting of Yale Students for Christ and the Yale Humanist Community. I appreciate all of the discussion in these places.

Others who gave comments or encouragement include A. J. Roberts, Samuel Loncar, Priscilla Guerra, John Hare, Tony and Katie Bomkamp, Michael and Ansley Swanson, David and Karen Mahan, Rick and Soozie Schneider, Jon and Anita Hinkson, Don and Sue Smedley, Dave and Deb Horner, Kerri Thorn, Dave Peterson, and Ben Northrup.

Lizzy Ganssle, Tony Bomkamp, Steven Horst, and Kevin Timpe each read the entire manuscript with great care. They gave extensive comments. I have taken most of their suggestions, and I take responsibility for not following them all. I also want to thank David McNutt, my editor at InterVarsity Press. His comments were helpful, and his entire team made this book what it is.

My family—Jeanie, David, Nick, and Lizzy—provided encouragement and constant cheering. Three lifelong friends have been strong pillars over the decades. We all met the summer of 1978 and have tracked with each other since then. Dave Horner and I discovered and pursued philosophy in parallel tracks. After thirty-five years we finally teach in the same department. This situation brings great joy. Dave Kanne helped me from the earliest years of my work in campus ministry to be confident to lead and to teach. Kurt Richardson is the most consistent, thoughtful friend a person could have. He regularly reminds me of the milestones in our shared journey. The encouragement of these three has helped make me the person I am today. They have been a steady reminder that, as the psalmist says,

> Behold, you have made my days a few handbreadths,
> and my lifetime is as nothing before you.
> Surely all mankind stands as a mere breath! (Ps 39:5 ESV)

It is fitting and a pleasure to dedicate this book to these friends.

Introduction

MAKING SENSE OF OUR DESIRES

I always had a sense of dread when exams were handed back in class. What was my grade? Was I in deep trouble or only minor trouble? If I was in deep trouble, my mind turned to the second worry: Can I pass the class? Imagine my surprise when I saw a B on my calculus exam. I was safe. As the instructor went through the problems on the test, however, I became more and more restless. Perhaps I was not safe after all. It began to feel like trouble. The way he explained the problem did not match what I had written, yet I had received a significant amount of credit. After class I approached him, handed him my test, and asked a question he had probably never heard. "Can you look at question 3 and tell me what I did *right*?" He walked through the steps and explained how I was actually on the right track. I did get a B. I was not in trouble after all!

Calculus does not make sense to me. It never has. If I had worked harder, it might have turned out differently. But I didn't work at it. I never learned it. Almost forty years later, all I remember is the feeling of dread and wondering what I did right. But calculus is not the only thing that does not make sense to me.

Not long after I finished college, I spent a summer in Ocean City, New Jersey. Down the street from where I stayed was a delicatessen called Ed's Deli. I would be surprised if it is still there. My friends and I would stop in most days and buy junk food. (I was younger then. I still buy junk food, but now I feel guilty about it.) One day there was a long line for checkout. As I waited I took a few strings of penny licorice out of the jar on the counter and ate them. This was in 1982, and the licorice did cost a penny a string! As I paid for my snacks, I said, "Here's three cents for the licorice." The teenage girl behind the counter exclaimed about my honesty. Why would I pay for something I could have eaten for free? I said, "Well, my integrity is worth more than three cents." It never occurred to me to take the licorice without paying. Stealing candy does not make sense.

So among the things that do not make sense to me are calculus and shoplifting. These two items fail to make sense in very different ways. Calculus does not make sense because it is too complicated. Shoplifting is different. It does not make sense to me, but I understand it exactly. There is no confusion. Its lack of sense is of a different kind altogether. It does not make sense because I cannot fit it into what I know about who I am and what I want my life to be. Something makes sense in this way if it fits with what we believe or care about. It does not make sense if it does not fit. There is a kind of connection when things make sense in this way. What connects with what we hold to be true or important makes sense. What does not connect does not make sense.

Each human being has a project. In fact, we all share the same project. This project is to navigate the world in the best way we can. Each of us proceeds with the aim of being and doing certain things but not others. We aim to do the things that make sense to us and to avoid the things that don't. We navigate the world in light of our commitments and assumptions about what is good to do or to be. These commitments determine what makes sense to us and what does not.

Small events or decisions make sense if they connect with a bigger view of our life and do not make sense if they do not connect. Thus the larger questions shape the smaller ones.

I try to make this point in some of the philosophy classes I teach. I write on the board this question: "What sort of person should I be?" I explain that this is *the* central philosophical question. It touches every major area of philosophy. The question opens inquiry about what sorts of things human beings are. What sort of world do we live in? How do we know about this world? The question connects to concerns about moral reality. Is there moral reality, and what is it like? How can we know about it? Is there a God, and if so, how does God matter to us? How can we live well together?

The question of what kind of person one should be is not theoretical. Your answer to this question affects how you navigate your life. Each person lives in a way that is based on his answer to that question. It is not that we think about the answer explicitly, but the way that we would answer it explains how we approach everything else. We may theorize about this question in the classroom, but we actually wrestle with it in the trenches of our day-to-day experience. Each of us answers this question with some idea of what the better life is. How we think about the good life reflects, among other things, our deeper assumptions about what it means to be a human being.

The question of the kind of person I should be leads to two others: What sort of person do I *want* to be? And what sort of person am I *becoming*? Coming to grips with the first of these two questions helps me discover my deeper desires and commitments. The second reminds me that I am surely becoming one sort of person or another. I am in process of becoming the person I will be.

It is striking how rarely we reflect on how our choices, habits, and patterns influence the kind of person we become. Our culture suffers from what I call *moral atomism*. Moral atomism is the assumption that each choice we make is largely independent of all our other choices.

We think that our ability to decide is fresh and unhindered at each fork in the road we face. Like the ancient atomists who thought that the basic particles that make up reality were independent and interacted only by bumping into each other, we tend to think that each choice we make is isolated from every other choice. The truth of the matter is that each of our choices makes us either more or less able to make the right choices in the future. We train ourselves in our abilities to recognize and do what we think we ought to do.

The assumptions by which we navigate our lives include more than what we *believe*. They include our desires or our *loves*. It is not only what I think is true that will affect how I pursue the best life. It is also what I most want. What kind of person do I want to be? That question reveals my deeper desires. Augustine wrote that when it comes to our moral and spiritual well-being, what we want is actually more important than what we believe: "For when there is a question as to whether a man is good, one does not ask what he believes, or what he hopes, but what he loves."[1] He articulates this further: "So that it seems to me that it is a brief but true definition of virtue to say, it is the order of love."[2] A good person loves the right things and also loves them in the right order. The root of moral and spiritual failure, Augustine thought, is that our loves are disordered. He would say that our moral failures are not a result of our loving bad things. Rather, we love good things, but we love the less important things more than the most important things. Other philosophers have agreed with this thought. For example, Kant affirms that the pursuit of happiness is a good thing and that in the long run our happiness and our duty coincide. But we have a tendency to act in the short run for our own happiness rather than to do what we

---

[1]Augustine, *Enchiridion*, trans. J. F. Shaw, in *Nicene and Post-Nicene Fathers*, ed. Philip Schaff, first series (1887; repr., Peabody, MA: Hendrickson, 2003), 3:274.

[2]Augustine, *City of God*, trans. Marcus Dods, in *Nicene and Post-Nicene Fathers*, first series, 2:303.

ought. This pattern marks the propensity to evil that is a pervasive part of human experience.[3]

It does not take a philosopher to help us see this principle. We recognize that few people set out trying to be evil. People usually aim to do or to pursue something that seems good to them. Where we go wrong is that we pursue one good at the expense of other goods. Often we pursue our own interests, which may be good in themselves, at the expense of our duties to other people. Whenever I am honest, I recognize that I act in this way.

Each person, then, has her own collection of beliefs and loves. Although they may seem to be tangled together with no conscious structure, a little self-reflection can lead us to recognize that there is a rough order to our loves and beliefs. Certain loves take precedence over others. We are prompted to self-reflection when we experience conflicts among our beliefs and our loves. These conflicts are experiences of *dissonance*. Dissonance is the sensed tension between two things we want to continue to hold. Whenever we experience dissonance, we strive to resolve the conflict.

Cognitive dissonance is tension that arises when our beliefs come into conflict with each other. I often experience this tension when I try to find my keys. I believe I left them on the counter next to my wallet, but they are not there. I have one belief based on my memory and another based on the fact that I don't see them where I expect to see them. These beliefs conflict with each other. I want to find my keys, but I also want to find an explanation for the dissonance. Why were the keys not where I thought they would be? I keep looking for a resolution. If I figure out the problem, I feel a sense of relief. Finding my keys is a simple case. Cognitive dissonance in other cases can be deep and persistent. Scholars sifting through complex evidence face a

---

[3]Immanuel Kant, *Religion Within the Bounds of Reason Alone*, ed. Robert M. Adams (Cambridge: Cambridge University Press, 1999).

deeper kind of cognitive dissonance. It often takes a great deal of time to work out their ideas and find resolution.

When we have difficulty deciding what we should do, we are faced with *practical* dissonance. Practical dissonance occurs when our desires come into conflict with one another or with some of our beliefs. Some instances of practical dissonance are moral, and some are not. For example, when I drive I often *feel* sure of which way I should go. I know that my wife's sense of direction is better than mine, so when Jeanie says "turn left," I experience practical dissonance. What should I do? The question is not always a matter of simple cognitive dissonance. I am not merely trying to figure out the best way to get where I am going. To be honest, I also do not want to be wrong. I think I ought to turn right, and I want to be correct about that. I have also learned that Jeanie is right more than I am, so I also think that I ought to turn left. Having learned to trust Jeanie more than my own sense of direction, I usually follow her instructions. And it is a good thing too. This is a case of practical dissonance that is not especially moral. Of course, if I get frustrated or angry, it might *become* a moral issue!

Moral dissonance may arise when you are standing in a long line at the deli deciding whether to pay for the licorice you have already eaten. A little extra money is desirable, but doing the right thing is a deep value. What you think you ought to do is in conflict with something you might want. To pay for the candy is to choose that your moral value is more important than gaining a few cents.

When we experience dissonance, we strive for resolution. We want to remove the tension. We cannot remain in a state of conflict for significant periods of time. We achieve resolution by revising either the content of our beliefs and desires or by revising the ordering of our beliefs and desires. We will often change our beliefs to fit our loves. We are less ready to change our loves to fit our beliefs.

Advertisers are well aware that our values are deeper than our beliefs. I remember being in Leningrad in 1986, before the term *glasnost* had been coined. We sneaked one of our Russian friends into the hard-currency store. These were stores that took only Western money and allowed only Westerners to enter. On one wall of the store was a huge cigarette advertisement. It must have been thirty feet wide and ten feet tall. There was a beautiful picture of a man kayaking down a rushing mountain river amid thick green forest growth. In the bottom-right corner there was a picture of a pack of cigarettes. Our friend had never seen an advertisement of this sort. The only billboards in the Soviet Union at the time were propaganda signs for the Communist Party.

"You see, Arkosha," I explained, "the picture of the kayaker evokes a *mood* or a desire to be a certain kind of person. Then that mood or desire is associated with the brand of cigarette. The design of the ad has the aim of getting me to think, 'I am an adventurous sort of person. I should smoke Marlboro.'"

Arkosha was dumbfounded. "Do you mean that Americans will really buy things because of this?" he asked. He could not believe it.

"We fall for it all the time."

You can see that Augustine is right when he says that what we love tends to lie deeper, and be more important, than what we believe. No one *thinks consciously* that a certain brand of cigarettes gives you a more adventurous life than another brand. If someone claimed to present evidence for this claim, you would laugh. Yet, our desire for such a life can lead us to associate the two. What we want to be affects our decisions. What we want is usually deeper than what we believe, even if *some* of our beliefs may be deeper than some of our desires. In any given case of dissonance, we tend to retain what lies deeper. We revise what is more shallow.

At the heart of each person is the very deepest region of the self. I call this region, for lack of a better term, our *core identity*. A person's core identity involves the deepest sense the person has of who the person is and who the person longs to be. What constitutes our core identity is rarely in the forefront of our minds. Often it takes patient self-reflection and work to identify the contours of one's core identity. In some cases, it takes the help of friends or even a professional psychologist for us to recognize our own deepest sense of who we are and how that sense shapes what we do.

One's core identity often serves as the fulcrum for changes in one's other values. Deep value change will usually occur along the contours of core identity. I will change how I order my loves if the change of order conforms to this contour. When I find that I have reversed the order of my loves, I can usually trace the change to some aspect of my core identity. The function of one's core identity as a fulcrum is rarely conscious. Rather, we find certain values or beliefs simply gaining or losing their grip on us. If we trace this reordering carefully, we will find that some deeper love or some sense of who we are is at work.

The notion that each of us has a core identity raises two important questions. First, how is it that our core identities are formed? Second, how do our core identities change? The picture I have presented up to this point seems to imply that our core identities are fixed and cannot change. This notion cannot be right. The distinguishing marks of our core identities involve two things. First, our core identity involves those deeper beliefs and values that concern our self-understanding. Second, these deeper beliefs and values tend to persist over time. They concern the way we aim to place ourselves in the world as we understand it. They capture our deepest desires about the kind of persons we hope to be and our settled sense of who we are. So our core identities are not different in kind from our other beliefs and values. One's core identity consists of those beliefs and values that play a deeper role than others. We shape the rest of our beliefs and values around our core identity.

Our core identities are formed as we inhabit certain belief and value structures over time. We begin to inhabit beliefs and values at a very young age. In fact, we begin this process before we can speak. Our sense of being loved and of being secure has a great impact on our deepest sense of who we are. As we grow, we develop patterns of ordering our choices, other beliefs, values, goals, and interests around these deeper ones. It is in this way that we must ask what kind of persons we are becoming. Each time we adapt our surface beliefs and values to our deeper ones, the deeper ones become even more deeply entrenched. As a result, we become more fixed as a certain kind of person. In a sense, we *habituate* ourselves into our core identities by the practice of changing our other beliefs and values in light of them.

Given this account, we can see how it is possible to undergo changes in our core identities. This kind of change will often result from the experience of dissonance. Sometimes an event triggers a sudden confrontation with this dissonance. Other times we become aware of it gradually through conscious reflection. In either case, we may determine that some belief or desire that functioned within our core identity ought to be revised in light of other beliefs and desires. We may recognize that we have a deeply ingrained habit that we want to change. This habit may be revealed in our relationships with others or our thoughts about our own lives. Beginning such change will be difficult, in part, because we are changing *against* the contour of our deeper values. We have to rehabituate ourselves to inhabit a new ordering of values and beliefs.

We can call dissonance involving this deepest level *existential* dissonance. Existential dissonance occurs when who we want to be, at the deepest level, comes into conflict with other values or beliefs. We may be confronted with facts about who we actually are that conflict with our sense of who we want to be.

Jane Austen's character Emma provides a good illustration of how a sudden experience of existential dissonance can lead to a renovation of core identity. On a picnic to Box Hill with her friends, Emma makes a cruel joke at the expense of Miss Bates. Mr. Knightley chastises her strongly for the public insult because Miss Bates is poor and has no future prospects. When he challenges her, she is confronted with the realization that she is not the person she wants to be, nor the person she thought she was:

> While they talked, they were advancing towards the carriage; it was ready; and, before she could speak again, he had handed her in. He had misinterpreted the feelings which had kept her face averted, and her tongue motionless. They were combined only of anger against herself, mortification, and deep concern. . . . She was vexed beyond what could have been expressed—almost beyond what she could conceal. Never had she felt so agitated, mortified, grieved, at any circumstance in her life. She was most forcibly struck. The truth of his representation there was no denying. She felt it at her heart. How could she have been so brutal, so cruel to Miss Bates![4]

Mr. Knightley forced Emma to recognize that she had become the kind of person who was ready to hurt those of less standing than herself. She did not know that she had become that person. The recognition was shocking because it revealed dissonance in her deepest identity. Faced with this realization, she was crushed. The experience of existential dissonance can be powerful. Emma chooses to act almost immediately. She begins to practice showing real compassion. This practice helps her begin the difficult journey of change. She moves from being a person who is willing to show merely an expected amount of charity to those below her to a person who is no longer deeply concerned with the claims of rank. She faced who she was and put into practice the action that could reshape her core identity.

[4]Jane Austen, *Emma*, ed. R. W. Chapman, 3rd ed., The Novels of Jane Austen 4 (London: Oxford University Press, 1933), 375-76.

This brief description of our beliefs, loves, and identities is not meant to be a comprehensive moral psychology. It is meant to help us think about what it means for something to make sense to us. As I mentioned in the opening paragraphs of this chapter, the way that calculus makes sense is different from the way one's commitment to a certain kind of life makes sense. The claim that I ought not to steal a few pieces of candy or cheat on my taxes is one that makes sense to me in the manner I am exploring here. It fits in neatly with things I believe and value deeply. Integrity in my financial life connects to the person I want to be and the person I think I am. The connection or fittingness of integrity with my core identity explains why honesty makes sense to me.

The claim that this book will explore is that the Christian story makes sense of our deepest longings. That is, the story that Christianity sets forth fits well with the things we value most and with the kinds of people we want to be. The Christian story has the resources to ground these desires. It can explain why we have the aspirations we do, and it can show that these aspirations connect with what is real.

My claim might strike some readers as odd. To many people, Christianity is associated with narrow-mindedness and judgmental attitudes. These qualities do not fit at all with the kinds of people we want to be. To the degree that it might promote these things, Christianity will *not* make sense of who we want to be. Undoubtedly, some people who are Christians are narrow-minded or judgmental. These flaws are found throughout the population. Christianity itself, however, is a story about reality. It holds forth a particular picture of reality. This picture includes the purposes and the nature of God, as well as the nature of the world that God made. I will argue that it is *this picture* that makes sense of who we are and what we want most. I will reveal that there is a tight connection between Christianity and features of our deepest aspirations, even if there are Christians who do not seem to recognize these connections. Our deepest loves and values seem to reflect human nature itself. Christianity, I hope to show, makes a great deal of sense when it is considered in the context of these human concerns.

It is important for me to make it clear that I shall not argue that Christianity is *true*. I believe it is true, but for most people, the question of whether it is true is not the most important question. My suspicion is that there are many people who think something like the following: "I am pretty sure that Christianity is not true, and it is a good thing that it is not." I want to challenge the second part of this thought. I hope to persuade readers that it would be a good thing if Christianity turned out to be true. For this reason, I will explore elements of our experience that we care deeply about, and I will point out how the Christian picture of reality makes sense of these elements.

In the course of this discussion, I will periodically compare the way that the Christian story connects with these elements to the way that various atheistic stories connect. Different worldviews set forth different pictures of what reality is like. We navigate the world in terms of our views about what is real and what is most important. It is certainly the case that Christianity and atheism are not the only alternatives on the market. Furthermore, there are a wide variety of versions of each of these worldviews. I will restrict my comments about the relative fittingness of worldviews to Christianity and atheism because these represent two of the more prevalent worldviews in the West. Furthermore, atheism dominates the cultural institution within which I spend most of my time: the university. I think atheism is the leading competitor, even if it is not the only competitor, to Christianity.

In explaining the Christian story, I will from time to time quote from both the Old and New Testaments. Although Christians hold the Scripture to have religious authority, I do not cite these texts in this way. I do not ask the reader to believe something because it is stated in the Scriptures. As indicated above, my primary goal here is not to ague for the truth of certain claims or positions or texts. I use these texts to explain features of the Christian story.

I recognize as well that it is dangerous to talk about *our* core identities and *our* deepest values. It assumes that there are widely shared features among people's core identities. I do make these assumptions because I think they are true. At the same time, I recognize that values, features of core identities, and the ordering of loves are not *universally* shared, even if they may be widely shared. You may not agree with what I claim about the contours of our core identities. My argument for the claim that Christianity connects with what we think to be most important may not resonate as strongly with you. If you recognize your own deep values in what I discuss, you may see that, indeed, Christianity makes a good deal of sense.

Part I

PERSONS

One

PERSONS AND HAPPINESS

Long ago, Aristotle observed that everyone acts for some aim or goal. Concerning this goal, he says, "Most people, I should think, agree about what it is called, since both the masses and sophisticated people call it happiness."[1] Everyone agrees that the goal is happiness. If we try to think about what it means to be happy or what the ingredients of happiness might be, it gets more complicated. Aristotle goes on to say, "They disagree about substantive conceptions of happiness, the masses giving an account which differs from that of the philosophers."[2]

Everyone wants to be happy. People have always wanted to be happy. We all want to be happy, but we do not want happiness at any cost. Philosopher John Stuart Mill quips, "It is better to be a human being dissatisfied than a pig satisfied; better to be Socrates dissatisfied than a fool satisfied."[3] Mill does not provide an abstract defense for

---

[1]Aristotle, *Nicomachean Ethics*, trans. Roger Crisp (Cambridge: Cambridge University Press, 2000), book 1, chap. 4, 1095a, 16-18.

[2]Ibid., book 1, chap. 4, 1095a, 20-21.

[3]John Stuart Mill, *Utilitarianism*, ed. George Sher, 2nd ed. (Indianapolis: Hackett, 2001), 10.

this claim. He merely states, "And if the fool, or the pig, are of a different opinion, it is because they only know their own side of the question. The other party to the comparison knows both sides."[4] In other words, to anyone who understands what it is to be a human being, it will be obvious that it is better to be a human being, even if one is dissatisfied, than to be a well-satisfied pig.

Mill recognized that a happy pig has its needs and desires fulfilled, while a sad human being does not. He is claiming that there is something more important than having our needs and desires satisfied. Mill's claim is significant because his book is a defense of utilitarianism. Utilitarianism is the ethical view that the right action to do is the one that brings the most pleasure to the most people, counting each person the same. Happiness consists in pleasure, and, for utilitarians, pleasure is the only thing that is intrinsically good. Pain is the only intrinsic bad. As far as our moral thinking is concerned, it does not matter whether it is simple physical pleasure or psychological, aesthetic, or intellectual pleasure. Any pleasure counts. Why, then, does Mill think it is better to be a dissatisfied human being than to be a fully satisfied pig?

Mill thought that pleasure is the only intrinsic good. He disagreed with some other utilitarian philosophers, however, because he thought that although any pleasure counts, not all pleasures are equal. All pleasures are valuable, but some pleasures are more valuable than others. The *quantity* of pleasure was not the only morally relevant issue. Pleasures can be compared in terms of their *qualities* as well. If the quantity of pleasure is the only thing that matters, then a happy pig might be better off than a sad person.

Whether or not you think utilitarianism is right, you probably think Mill is correct in his claim that the amount of pleasure one has is not the only important thing about life. Although Mill illustrates this

---

[4]Ibid.

notion with his talk of the qualities of pleasures, most of us will think that his distinction does not go far enough. We value some things more than pleasure. Happiness is too complex and rich a concept to be reduced to the quantity and the quality of our pleasures.

We can illustrate this idea by considering friendship. Think about what one of your friends wants for you. Your friend wants you to be happy. But your friend wants more for you than happiness. A good friend will not be content simply if you have pleasure. Your friend wants you to have a *good* life. She will want you to be well satisfied, but she will also want your life to be *worthy* of your satisfaction. To be a friend is to want what is best for the other. Your friend will not be content if you are satisfied with unworthy things. This fact about friendship explains why it saddens us when our friends make bad choices. We want our friends to flourish because, deep down, we have the conviction that becoming the best person we can become brings the best quality of life. We want our friends to have the best life they can have. As we reflect on friendship, then, we see that having the greatest amount of pleasure is not the most important thing to us.

Mill points out that human beings have far greater capacities than other animals to experience a wide range of pleasures. It is our being human that opens our horizons for experiencing the quality of life to which we aspire. We can see, then, why Mill claims that it is better to be a dissatisfied human being than to be a perfectly satisfied pig. For Mill, the ability to experience greater qualities of pleasure is tied to the capacities we have because we are persons. He observes, "Human beings have faculties more elevated than the animal appetites and, when once made conscious of them, do not regard anything as happiness which does not include their gratification."[5] Mill recognizes that it is our humanness that gives us our deepest desires, and it is our humanness that gives us the capacity to fulfill them.

---

[5]Ibid., 8.

Again, a little reflection shows that Mill is right about the connection between being human and the variety of pleasures we can have. We value, among other things, having enriching experiences, gaining wisdom and knowledge, receiving and expressing love, interpersonal communication, and joy. Each of these presupposes the existence of faculties more elevated than those we find in other animals. Human beings are the sort of beings that can experience these things that we value. While it is true that other animals can have experiences, the value of our experiences to ourselves is enhanced because we are aware of ourselves experiencing the good things we encounter. This awareness is connected to the kind of consciousness thought to be a mark of personhood.

One thing we learn from Mill, then, is that what we value most is connected to our personhood. In fact, almost everything we value in life is tied to persons. The value of the things we pursue for ourselves is enhanced because we have human capacities, and we value other people intrinsically. Mill's insight helps us see why it is that the central questions of life are about what it means to be a person.

Two

PEOPLE MATTER MOST

September 11, 2001, left a mark on our shared consciousness. All of America, and much of the world, was glued to its television sets. We simply could not fathom the images we saw. We faced horror on such a large scale that we could not conceive it. Not since the Kennedy assassination or perhaps Pearl Harbor had our nation been so stunned. The memories are burned into our minds and hearts. Those who were old enough to be aware at the time will never forget that day.

In the aftermath of that tragedy, certain things became clear. On that day, no one grieved for the loss of the buildings. The World Trade Center Towers were magnificent, beautiful buildings. They were marvels of engineering. But we did not grieve for them. Only later did we miss the buildings and feel sorrow over the change in the skyline of New York. That day we grieved for the people.

When the passengers on United Flight 93 realized that their plane had been hijacked, they scrambled for their phones. One commentator noted, in retrospect, that no one called the office to check on work. Everyone called the people they loved. They called to express their love. They called for one last connection. They called to say *goodbye*. Years later, we still mourn. We are still bewildered by those bizarre events. The loss of so many people in such a seemingly meaningless way stuns us.

We are a people of monuments. We feel compelled to mark the tragedies of our lives. When those tragedies are shared, we mark them publicly. We do not commemorate these events only because of our hurt or our sorrow or our unanswered questions. We commemorate 9/11 and other events like it because of the value we place on people. We remember them—we feel we must remember them—because people matter. Our shared tragedies remind us that people matter most.

That people matter most is something we rarely consciously think about. It is a deep commitment that almost everyone shares. Reflecting on this commitment suggests a question about reality. What kind of picture of reality makes room for the fact that people matter most? I suggest that the Christian picture of reality makes good sense of this aspect of our lives. In other words, the picture of reality presented by Christianity grounds and explains our values and aspirations concerning the importance of people. A simple observation is enough to show this claim to be true: *In the Christian story, the most fundamental reality is personal.*

Personhood is at the center of the Christian story. To say that God is real is to admit that God is the ultimate ground of the universe. God is not *within* the universe, but God is its source. Everything else depends on God, and God does not depend on anything else. This dependence is captured in the idea that God is the creator of the universe. When I talk about God as creator, I mean the fact that, in the Christian view, God brought the universe and everything in it into existence, and God keeps things in existence. I am not concerned with how or when God brought things into existence. There are many ways that God could have done it. There are Christian views in which God guided the evolutionary process intentionally, and there are views in which God creates more directly at various points. The most important piece of this idea is that the universe is the purposeful product of a personal being.

In the Christian understanding, God is personal. God is not a force, as in the Star Wars universe. God has the kind of features that are typical of personhood, including the capacity to know things, to act for reasons, to have preferences, and a moral nature. The Christian story includes the idea that everything that exists is the product of the activity of this divine, personal being. Reality, then, is personal at its root.

The claim that the most fundamental reality is personal is not unique to Christianity. It is shared by any position that holds that God exists and created the universe. Thus this understanding is held by the major monotheistic religions (Judaism, Christianity, and Islam). It is shared as well by some other religious theories, such as deism. All these positions agree that God is personal. If personhood is central in this way to these views, what difference does it make to how we navigate the world?

If it is really the case that the most fundamental reality is personal and everything depends on that being's action, then the universe is a created thing. Throughout this book we will think about implications of this claim in a variety of ways. Here we will focus on how the universe was made by God, who is good. Because God is good, God made the universe for good reasons. That God made the universe for good reasons shows that the world is not an accident. It is something done on purpose. Because there is some plan behind it, the universe has value. It is not superfluous. God is both brilliant and good. We are not surprised to see marks of these qualities in the universe. We should expect, then, that we will find it extremely interesting and beautiful and worthy of our care. And this is exactly what we find.

God's goodness grounds and explains the intrinsic goodness of the universe. This part of the Christian story explains why theistic ethical systems have always strongly affirmed the goodness of the created world. There are many worldviews or philosophies that affirm the opposite. Plato argued that the physical world, when compared to the Forms, was both less real than and more distant from the good. He thought that time, space, and the body were things that entrapped the soul. Death was liberation from the physical world. These ideas lie behind Socrates's claim that "the one aim of those who practice philosophy in the proper manner is to practice for dying and death."[1] By turning away from physical things and by contemplating the Forms, a philosopher frees himself as much as possible from the physical world. Some kinds of Gnosticism combined views influenced by Plato with the Christian idea of sin to posit that the physical world was intrinsically evil. Similar notions are found in some schools of Hinduism. The spiritual life, on all of these views, is an attempt to escape the physical world. The Christian picture of reality, however, affirms the idea that the physical world is good. It is made by a good God, and it is to be explored and enjoyed.

Not only is the universe a created thing, but in the Christian story human beings are also created things. God has specific reasons for creating us. As a result, the presence of persons in the universe also is not accidental. We came into being because a good and wise God saw fit to bring us into being. This forethought concerning persons does not apply only to the human species as a whole. It also applies to each person. No human being, on the Christian view, is an accident. God purposefully brought us into existence. You and I have been made for reasons by a powerful and good God.

That we are made by God guarantees that each human life is both valuable and meaningful in an objective sense. Our value is a matter of our *worth* in the cosmic scheme of things. Our meaning is a matter of there being a *point* to our existence. Regardless of how we feel about our worth, God has bestowed great value on us. The value that any human person has is given to her. It is not something that she has to achieve. It is not due to accidental or contingent factors, such as our health or education or whatever good we may do in the world. Each

[1]Plato, *Phaedo* 64a, in *Plato: Five Dialogues*, trans. G. M. A. Grube (Indianapolis: Hackett, 1981).

person has intrinsic value regardless of these things because each person is made by God for God's good reasons. The point to our existence is not a matter of our accomplishing anything or of our succeeding at some task. We fit into reality because we were made by God. Thus we matter.

We did not invent God's reasons for creating us, nor did anyone else. Therefore, these reasons cannot be erased or canceled by any human being. There is nothing that one human being can do to annul the real objective value of another human being. We may try to ignore or avoid the fact that a person's value is not up to us, but we cannot change this basic fact. There have been many attempts to ground human value in culture or in status or even in the state. Others try to locate the value of persons in their contribution to the broader society. If a person's worth is grounded in these kinds of things, either she may fail to gain value, or her value can be rescinded. We have seen throughout history that the claim that the value of certain people can be eliminated by others has catastrophic consequences. Because our value is derived from God's purposes, however, it cannot be overruled by any human being. The conviction that each person has intrinsic, objective, and indelible value has grounded the commitment to universal human rights.

In the Christian story, God has purposes for our existence, and therefore our existence has meaning as well as value. There is a point to our lives, and this point is grounded in something outside us as individuals and as communities, and even outside our membership in the biological species. Thus our meaning is objective, and it is independent of how we think our lives are going. Because God has purposes for us, our meaning does not depend on how we feel about our lives on any given day.

It is one of the persistent quests of each human being to achieve and experience a meaningful life. We want our work to be meaningful both to us and, in some way, beyond ourselves. We want to make a real contribution to others. We long to see that the things we do make other people's lives better. In short, we want to matter. Sometimes we succeed and can look at this part of our lives with a kind of satisfaction. Other times what we do or fail to do makes it hard to believe that we matter very much. If it depended on our accomplishments alone, the meaning of our lives would fluctuate with our success. We would put the burden of securing meaning on our performance. This burden is one that our performance, no matter how good it might be, cannot bear.

In the Christian story, we matter independently of our achievements. Our lives are meaningful simply because God has reasons for making us. We stand in relation to the fundamental meaning maker of the universe. The point of our lives is grounded in our relationship with God, and it is real whether we recognize it or not. We have been made and placed in this world for God's purposes. Although our accomplishments are fragile, our meaning is secure.

Not only do our lives have value and meaning, but our capabilities have value and meaning as well. It is another aspect of the Christian picture of reality that we reflect God. Human nature is a picture or image of God's own nature. Not every kind of theism holds this view. It is a claim that is held especially by those worldviews that adopt the first few chapters of Genesis as an authoritative story about the nature of human beings. There we find the claim that "God created humankind in his image, in the image of God he created them" (Gen 1:27). Historically, the most common understanding of what it means to be made in God's image has involved the *nature* of the human person.[2] The various capacities we share are reflections of God's own capacities. As a result, they too are intrinsically valuable. Because they are found in the nature of God, they are not accidental, and they have their own meaning and grounding.

---

[2] I will discuss other understandings of our being made in God's image below.

For example, the human ability to know true things about the world reflects God's own nature as a knowing being. God knows everything that can be known. Our capacities for knowledge reflect God's. To be sure, our knowledge is limited and fallible, but our quest to learn and our enjoyment of discovery have value beyond what we get out of them. They have intrinsic value because they are a function of the proper use of the capacities given to us in order that we might reflect God. We begin with questioning, searching, and wondering about reality. These habits mature into more sophisticated explorations through research, education, and the development of technology. All of these pursuits are reflections of God, and therefore they are appropriate human pursuits.

Another human capacity that reflects the nature of God is that human beings are agents. We have the ability to act in the world. We are not simply links in a chain of events; we make a difference. We can introduce new chains of events into the world. This feature reflects God's agency. God acted in bringing the universe into being, and God acts within it to accomplish the divine plan. We act as well. One outcome of this human feature is that in the Christian story what we do matters. Our choices and actions make a real difference. That God is the Creator and that we are made in God's image means that our work reflects the divine nature. Thus it has intrinsic value. It is not merely a means to other ends. Part of the divine plan is for human beings to bring good things out of the world into which we have been placed.

The Christian claim that the most fundamental reality is a personal being grounds the meaning and value of the entire cosmos, and especially human beings. God, being good, made us for good reasons. Furthermore, the capacities God has given us reflect the divine image. Human endeavors are infused with meaning.

In contrast to theistic views, the vast majority of atheistic views hold that whatever personhood exists arrived both very late in the history of the universe and completely by accident. As Bertrand Russell famously pronounced:

> That Man is the product of causes which had no prevision of the end they were achieving; that his origin, his growth, his hopes and fears, his loves and his beliefs, are but the outcome of accidental collocations of atoms; that no fire, no heroism, no intensity of thought and feeling, can preserve an individual life beyond the grave that all the labors of the ages, all the devotion, all the inspiration, all the noonday brightness of human genius, are destined to extinction in the vast heat death of the solar system, and that the whole temple of Man's achievement must inevitably be buried beneath the debris of a universe in ruins—all these things, if not quite beyond dispute, are yet so nearly certain, that no philosophy which rejects them can hope to stand. Only within the scaffolding of these truths, only on the firm foundation of unyielding despair can the soul's habitation henceforth be safely built.[3]

Russell's picture of reality is common, at least in its broad outline, to many versions of contemporary atheism. If atheism is true, as Russell indicates, persons arrived on the scene completely by accident. The most fundamental reality is not personal. It is matter and energy. There is no intrinsic direction for the processes of this fundamental feature except entropy. Whatever exists simply increases in disorder.

It is not that the emergence of life and, more specifically of human life, is impossible on this view. This claim is not necessary for the point I am making. But on Russell's view, it *is* surprising that the cosmos produced human beings, given its fundamental structure. There was no plan or foresight in the process. The fundamental structure of reality is indifferent to persons. Whether human beings come to exist

[3]Bertrand Russell, "A Free Man's Worship," in *Selected Papers of Bertrand Russell* (New York: Modern Library, 1927), 2-3. This essay was originally published in 1903.

or survive is completely accidental, as far as the way the universe works is concerned. On this cosmic scale, then, all human aspirations and virtues are accidental as well.

There is an element of despair in Russell's vision. We value most deeply the very qualities that are least at home in the world. The story that atheism puts forward is far less hospitable to the things we care about than the Christian story. I am not arguing here that Russell's view is *false*. It might turn out to be the true view of reality. Notice, however, that if it is true, there is a significant lack of fit between the way things are and our deepest sense of how they ought to be.

I also do not wish to claim that on Russell's view there is no value or meaning for persons. On an atheistic story, we can find meaning and great value. Our lives can be made rich through relationships and the pursuit of projects and causes that are important to us. Such meaning can and will be significant to us. We can come to value other people deeply. As Russell indicates, however, whatever personal meaning or value we find, on the atheistic view, is there *in spite of* the nature of reality rather than *because of* the nature of reality. It runs against the grain of the way things are, rather than along the contours of the way things are. Our meaning, though significant to us subjectively, is not connected to anything independent of human existence. Nor is it lasting or connected to any objective purpose outside ourselves.

We might distinguish between local meaning and cosmic meaning. The kind of meaning available in the atheistic story is local meaning. Think about the last time you played Monopoly. Every time you passed "Go" it was a happy event. The $200 you received was important. While you are playing the game, the money has meaning and value. You treat it as hard currency. You buy property and houses in order to make more money. You build your strategies around the value of the money. Within the game, the $200 matters. Once you stop playing the game, however, it all disappears. The five-hundred-dollar bill and the one-dollar bill have the same real value. Monopoly money has local value and local meaning. That is, it has value internal to the game, but no value or meaning external to it. If we agreed that each dollar of Monopoly money would be worth a dollar of *real* money, the values internal to the game would be grounded in values outside the game. In the atheistic picture of reality, human achievements and relationships have value and meaning locally, or internal to our social and psychological systems. Outside our chosen human structures, or cosmically, they have none.

On Russell's view, the various features of human life are also simply accidents. The quest for knowledge and understanding is important to us, but it is not connected to anything deeper in reality. Human agency and our moral natures also cut against the grain of the deep structure of reality. We can work to accomplish things, and we can choose to respect and help other people, but these aspirations are not well grounded. They are only internal to the game, and they do not last. Once the game is over, nothing remains. And, as Russell emphasizes, the game will end.

Although Russell was in no way a classic existentialist, this passage articulates themes that resonate with the projects of some of the leaders in that movement.[4] In a lecture delivered in Paris in 1945, Jean-Paul Sartre described the starting point of existentialism as Fyodor Dostoevsky's dictum "If God does not exist, everything is permitted."[5] While Dostoevsky announced this vision with dread,

---

[4]The following few paragraphs are revised from my essays "Consciousness, Memory, and Identity: The Nature of Persons in Three Films by Charlie Kaufman," in *Faith, Film, and Philosophy: Christian Reflections on Contemporary Film*, ed. James S. Spiegel and R. Douglas Geivett (Downers Grove, IL: InterVarsity Press, 2007), 106-21; and "Human Nature and Freedom in *Adaptation*," in *The Philosophy of Charlie Kaufman*, ed. David LaRocca (Lexington: University of Kentucky Press, 2011), 224-38.

[5]Jean Paul Sartre, *Existentialism and Humanism*, trans. Philip Mairet (London: Methuen, 1948). This lecture has been published with various titles, including the most literal: *Existentialism Is a Humanism*, trans. Carol Macomber (New Haven, CT: Yale University Press, 2007). It also has been published as *Existentialism*, trans. Bernard Frechtman (New York: Philosophical Library, 1947). My references are to *Existentialism and Humanism*.

Sartre thought it was the foundation of true freedom. It gives credence to the summary of Sartre's existential vision: *Existence precedes essence.* Sartre explains this quip by contrasting it with the Christian story, in which God has reasons for creating human beings, and these reasons provide the content of human nature. This content comprises the *essence* of a person. God then created with reference to this content. So the idea of a human being preceded the existence of any actual human beings. The idea of a human being was God's idea of what the nature of persons ought to be.

Sartre was explicitly rejecting this picture. He thought that there is no God and therefore that there is no human nature or essence at all. There are existing persons, and each person creates her own nature. People exist before they have any essence. In this way my nature is up to me. Sartre called this a radical freedom. There are no moral or divine boundaries limiting how I create my nature. My only obligation is to choose. Not to choose, that is, to allow unconsciously the culture around me to conform me into its own image, is to live in bad faith. Whatever life I live, I must choose it, and in doing so I create my nature. To choose my nature is my great dignity. I am responsible for what I am and what I become. For Sartre real values that are objective have disappeared along with God. Human beings are free. We are, in his words, "condemned to be free."[6] Sartre thought that people could not live without values. Thus we must *create* our own values. Furthermore, created values are only individual values. We cannot assess or even speak to the values that another person chooses to invent. Sartre saw his project as an attempt at a consistent atheism. He aimed to illustrate how it is possible to live in a way that is consistent with the sort of picture of reality that Russell and others have offered.

There is a sense in which the contrast between Russell and Sartre's stories, on the one hand, and the Christian story, on the other, is quite

---

[6]Sartre, *Existentialism and Humanism*, 34.

simple. On the Russell and Sartre view, there is no purpose or meaning prior to that which is made by human beings because there is no personal being prior to human persons. Values and meaning must be invented by existing human beings. Therefore, values and meaning are short-lived and destined for extinction. In the Christian view of reality, there is a personal being who exists prior to human persons. Furthermore, this personal God designed and created all other persons. As a result meaning and purpose are prior to and not dependent on the individual successes and failures of particular human beings. Our hopes and dreams are not destined to die, as Russell claims, "buried beneath the debris of a universe in ruins."

We find that persons are central to our lives. They matter most. How deep are persons in our picture of reality? We can see that the Christian story differs from the atheistic story at the core. The most fundamental reality, on the Christian view, is a personal God. We have been created to be persons, and people are what matter most to us. Persons are central to reality. The fit between our deepest longings and the Christian story is striking.

Three

WE FLOURISH IN RELATIONSHIPS

"Lord, what fools these mortals be!"[1] So Puck sizes up the dynamics of the human drive for love. Shakespeare's *A Midsummer Night's Dream* is a delightful romp through the anxieties and vicissitudes of romantic attachment. The fates of the main characters are controlled by Oberon, the king of the fairies. He capriciously casts spells to change their attachments, seemingly for his own entertainment. Through his intrigues, Lysander, Demetrius, Hermia, and Helena are tossed in and out of love. Which character is the current object of love of another is not under the control of any of the protagonists. The one constant feature that runs through their mishaps is their intense passion to be loved. Shakespeare tapped into a pervasive human desire. He knew that the longings of his characters would shine a light into the hearts of his audience.

Things have not changed in the centuries that have passed. The quest for love is as constant as ever. The enduring fascination with the novels of Jane Austen testifies to our love affair with love. Popular

---

[1]William Shakespeare, *A Midsummer Night's Dream*, act 3, scene 2, line 121.

culture is a celebration of this obsession. There is no end to the number of romantic comedies produced. Although their plots can be predictable, we still delight in the story of love discovered and love overcoming obstacles. Popular music overflows with the themes of love won and love lost. The power of pop music to shape our sense of self is lamented by Rob Gordon, a character in the film *High Fidelity*. In the midst of breaking up with his girlfriend, Gordon poses the question:

> What came first? The music or the misery? People worry about kids playing with guns and watching violent videos, we're scared that some sort of culture of violence is taking them over. . . . But nobody worries about kids listening to thousands—literally thousands—of songs about broken hearts and rejection and pain and misery and loss. Did I listen to pop music because I was miserable, or was I miserable because I listened to pop music?[2]

More subdued in its approach is the eighth book of Aristotle's *Nicomachean Ethics*, in which he treats friendship. He begins by acknowledging that friendship is "an absolute necessity in life."[3] While he acknowledges that some friendships are based on utility and pleasure, these kinds are only incidental. They are easily dissolved, and they tend to last only as long as the utility or the pleasure lasts. In contrast, "those who wish good things to a friend for his own sake are friends most of all, since they are disposed in this way towards each other because of what they are, not for any incidental reason."[4] This kind of friendship is lasting. He describes friendship as a state rather than a feeling. Friendship, then, involves a settled disposition to act for the good of

---

[2] *High Fidelity*, directed by Stephen Frears, screenplay by D. V. De Vincentis, Steve Pink, and John Cusack (Touchstone Pictures, 2000). Based on Nick Hornby, *High Fidelity* (New York: Riverhead Books, 1995). Transcript accessible at *The Internet Movie Script Database*, www.imsdb.com/scripts/High-Fidelity.html (accessed February 26, 2013).

[3] Aristotle, *Nicomachean Ethics*, trans. Roger Crisp (Cambridge: Cambridge University Press, 2000), book 8, 1155a, 5.

[4] Ibid., book 8, 1156b, 9-11.

the friend. While being loved is a universal and strong desire, "friendship seems to consist more in loving than in being loved."[5] Love, Aristotle claims, is the virtue of friendship. It is what makes a friendship more than incidental. Love makes a friendship excellent.

A Midsummer Night's Dream, *High Fidelity*, and *Nicomachean Ethics* are worlds apart in their aims, their literary approaches, and their philosophical outlook. Thinking about the range of such works, however, prompts a fundamental question about human nature and experience. What is it about us that makes us crave relationship? Our relationships are, without doubt, the most central aspects of our lives. Perhaps nothing on earth contributes more to our well-being than the experience and quality of our interpersonal relationships. Nothing can cause as profound a pain as loss or hurt on the relational level. Why are our relationships so central?

Our psychological and emotional development depends on the quality of our relationships. Our loving and our being loved—our knowing another and our being known by another—touches the depths of our core identity. The single most important influence on the development of our core identity is our relational environment. A parent's love and touch are crucial to the emotional well-being of a growing child. Without the concrete expression of this kind of love, a child develops serious psychological deficits. Emotional deprivation damages our core identities.

A little reflection helps us see that our capacity for relationship is connected with what it means to be a person. In order to enter into a relationship, we need capabilities that are largely unique to persons. In relationships, we *recognize* one another as selves rather than as objects. We see that other people have their own experiences, joys, and sorrows. As a result, we feel empathy, and we enter into the hopes and sorrows of another. We bond with each other such that your burdens become

---

[5]Ibid., book 8, 1159a, 26-27.

my burdens, and your joys become my joys. These pursuits require understanding, observation, and the ability to communicate. We use language and employ our intellect in our relationships. Ultimately, it is *because* we are persons that we can enter into and enjoy the richness of relationships.

Because we are persons, it is not just the case that we can enter into relationships; it is also the case that we *must* enter into relationships. Even if one cannot fail to have relationships, one may be impoverished with respect to the relationships one has. Relational poverty can be a result of a series of choices, or it can be a matter of unfortunate circumstances. From the poignant picture of loneliness in the song "Eleanor Rigby," who was "buried along with her name," to the isolation of Dickens's character Scrooge, we see that relational poverty is human poverty.[6] We are sad for those trapped in loneliness that is beyond their control, and we pity those who choose it for themselves. The financially successful businessman like Scrooge who has lost his family and friends on the road to success is a standard symbol of human failure.

Relationships are indeed central to our lives. This fact raises the question of where relationships fit in our picture of reality. Christianity holds forth a story that captures this centrality. The Christian story is relational at its core. The human capacity for relationship is a reflection of the divine capacity for relationship. This fact is one additional way in which human nature is a reflection of the divine nature. The features of our personhood that allow for and require human relationships are explained and grounded in the Christian picture of God as a personal being.

Human relationality, however, connects with Christianity in even deeper ways than the fact that we reflect God's own capacities for relationship. *In the Christian story, the most fundamental reality is*

[6]The Beatles, "Eleanor Rigby," by John Lennon and Paul McCartney, on *Revolver*, Sony/ATV Music Publishing, 1966.

intrinsically relational. This claim is part of the idea of the Trinity in the Christian view of God. Christianity teaches that there is one God in three persons. Each of the divine persons is of the same divine substance and has the same divine essence as the other divine persons. Thus there is one being. The persons of the Trinity, however, have their own individual personhood. This claim is the reason that Christians talk of God in terms of three in one. The Trinity is a distinctive contribution of Christianity. It is not shared by deism or the other major monotheistic religions. While various theisms hold that God has the capacity for relationship, it is a claim distinct to Christianity that relationality is part of God's very nature.

There are many mysterious elements in the concept of the Trinity, as we should expect in the nature of God. We will not raise these puzzles or try to defend the doctrine. Instead, we are interested in how this piece of the Christian picture of reality connects with our relationality. The notion that God exists as Trinity brings unique resources to our thinking. God eternally lives in relationship. Relationality, then, is as deep as the deepest feature of reality. It is not a feature that was added to reality as an afterthought. The most fundamental reality is not simply personal but a community of three persons in relationship.

Furthermore, the purpose for which God created us did not have to do with a lack in God's character or experience. God did not have to wait to create us in order to complete the divine relational capacities. God's ability to share in relationship was always complete. God experienced relationship from all eternity. Rather than creating us to meet a need on God's part, God created us for our own good. Creation is motivated by an overflowing of the love inherent in the very nature of God. That relationality reflects the deepest contours of reality resonates with our own experience of the centrality of relationship in our own lives.

Another theme that emerges from reflection on God's intrinsic relationality concerns the *manner* of the relations within the divine being. The manner of relation in the Trinity is one of mutual submission and cooperation. Theologian Hans Urs von Balthasar writes of "God's eternal self-emptying in the mutual self-surrender of the Persons of the Trinity."[7] Each divine person lives in eternal self-giving to the other divine persons. The mode of relationship is one of loving and giving. It is each self pouring the self out for others. Love is directed away from self and toward the other. Mutual love and giving are the deepest marks of the origin of relationship.

This feature of the relations within the Trinity captures our deep intuitions about the way relationships ought to be. We know that the best of our relationships are characterized by mutual giving. We all long for relationships in which we are known and accepted and supported while we in turn know, accept, and support the other. Furthermore, our greatest heroes are people who give themselves sacrificially for others. Figures such as Mother Teresa or Martin Luther King Jr. remind us of how self-sacrifice for the benefit of others can capture our affections and imaginations. We have the sense that their kind of life is the right kind of life. At our best, we aspire to live our lives in a similarly self-giving way. There is a deep fittingness, then, between what we grasp about the best in human relationships on the one hand and the manner of relating among the persons of the Trinity on the other. God's intrinsic being exemplifies what we were made to be.

God's love for the created order and particularly for the persons God created is an overflow of the love among the distinct persons within the divine nature. Love overflows into creative giving. When our first son, David, was born, I was amazed at the "love overflow" that we experienced. We had this brand-new, very little person in our home, and I remember thinking that the whole center of gravity of our lives had shifted. This shift was a matter of joy and celebration,

---

[7]Hans Urs von Balthasar, *Theo-Drama: Theological Dramatic Theory: The Last Act* (San Francisco: Ignatius, 1988), 243.

not of a burden. To be sure, our lives were thrown into chaos. It was a major accomplishment for one of us to finish a sentence. Despite the chaos, exhaustion, and anxiety of being new parents, the overwhelming experience was an overflow of love. When Nick was born twenty-two months later, the love overflow was just as strong. We found the same experience after three and a half more years when Lizzy came into our lives.

Once we reflect on the quality of relationship that characterizes God's own being, we are not surprised that the content of Christian ethics centers on love and service to others. Jesus continually stretched the moral imaginations of his followers in terms of whom they were to love. He named the second-most important law as the law to "love your neighbor as yourself" (Mt 22:39). When someone asked him, "And who is my neighbor?" (Lk 10:29), Jesus broke down the walls that had been erected to confine love. It is clear that the one who raised this question was seeking to limit the kind of people he was obligated to love. In response Jesus told the story that has come to be known as the parable of the good Samaritan. In it a man who was regarded as an outcast by those who were listening to the story crossed racial, religious, and cultural barriers to help a person in need. Jesus did not answer the question of the identity of our neighbor. Calculating whom it is that we are supposed to love, as if we can draw these kinds of boundaries, is to miss the point altogether. Rather, we should live as this man lived. We are to *be* neighbors who reach out to anyone in need.

Jesus pushed his followers even further: "You have heard that it was said, 'You shall love your neighbor and hate your enemy.' But I say to you, Love your enemies and pray for those who persecute you" (Mt 5:43-44). The self-giving love that expressed God's own nature among the persons of the Trinity and to us is to be our model of how we ought to love not just our family and friends, but those who are strangers and those who may be out to hurt us. To be honest, we have rarely seen anyone consistently come close to meeting the challenge of these commands. When we do witness such love, we tend to be humbled and awed. Self-sacrifice is hard, but it makes sense that this would be our ethical standard because self-giving reflects both the internal love within the Trinity and the external love God demonstrates toward us.

The Christian story, then, captures many of our deepest intuitions and aspirations about relationships. It makes sense of the fact that relationships are the most important aspect of our lives. It grounds even the manner in which we best relate and to whom we relate. Practicing this vision of relationship, then, results in the best quality of life for human beings.

If atheism is true, relationality is a shallow thing in the universe. Personhood and relationality are late arrivals and have emerged as pure accident. Most atheistic stories about how we came to value our relationships rely on an unguided Darwinian story. Darwinian explanations can be compatible with the Christian story as long as the process is not thought to be unguided. God's purposes in creating human beings require God's guidance in the process.

In the unguided story, our relational nature arises solely from our biological nature, which in turn arises from the underlying physics. In these accounts, the human drive to form and value relationships found its impetus in the need to survive. Groups of human beings that began to cooperate survived better than those groups that did not cooperate. That we value relationships is a cultural byproduct of the survival value of cooperation.[8] According to this view, the fundamental reality that gave rise to human relationship is *competition*. Competition on an individual level gave way to competition on a group level. Our cooperative relationships with those within our group emerged through competition with other groups. Cooperation had survival value only because it increased one group's ability to compete with other groups.

[8]Daniel Dennett provides an interesting discussion of these ideas in chap. 7 of his *Breaking the Spell: Religion as a Natural Phenomenon* (New York: Viking, 2006).

Dispositions towards loyalty and sacrifice are subsumed under a competitive framework. Our current deep valuing of love and sacrifice, then, is a bit of an anomaly. In this view, it originated purely for survival purposes.

On this view, the origin of our relationality is rooted in competition, yet this fact does not eliminate the meaning and value of relationship for us today. There is widespread agreement that love and sacrifice constitute moral virtues. Atheistic stories do allow us to recognize that relationships characterized by love and sacrifice contribute toward our flourishing. That our flourishing requires love, however, is an accident of evolutionary history. Our beliefs about these relational virtues do not track with the deep contours of reality. So, although the meaning and value of relationships are not incompatible with atheism, they do not fit as well into the atheistic story.

The lack of fit is found in the fact that things that are most important to us are least at home in the atheist universe. In navigating our lives along the lines of our relationships, we are swimming upstream. Relationality can be only as deep as personhood. In the atheistic story, personhood is a shallow thing. Thus relationality is shallow as well.

In the Christian story, the fundamental relational reality is marked by loving submission and by self-giving. Human cooperation and love do not find their origin in competition. These features find their origin and root in the deepest cooperation and love on a cosmic, divine level. That relationality plays this fundamental role in the human psyche is not surprising if Christianity is true. After all, relationality is at the core of the universe.

One of my favorite screenwriters is Charlie Kaufman. I have written two essays on his work.[9] He is best known for the films *Being John Malkovich* (1999), *Adaptation* (2002), and *Eternal Sunshine of the*

---

[9]See footnote 4 in chap. 2.

Spotless Mind (2004). What makes Kaufman's work fascinating to me is his persistent exploration of what it means to be a human being. In an online interview Kaufman commented on his writing. The context was a discussion of the film *Adaption*, which is framed around the search for orchids:

> Charlie Kaufman: I don't know what else there is to write about other than being human, or, more specifically, being this human. I have no alternative. Everything is about that, right? Unless it's about flowers.
>
> Rob Feld: Which turned out to be about what it is to be human.
>
> Charlie Kaufman: That's right.[10]

Kaufman's comment "Everything is about that" captures the centrality of personhood in our core identity. Even a film about orchids is really about being human. As we have explored personhood with the Christian story in mind, we have seen how our deepest core values and longings regarding persons resonate with Christianity. Christianity holds that we are made by God for good reasons and that our natures and our relational contours find resonance with God's own nature. In this way the Christian story grounds and explains *what* it is we care about most and *why* we care so deeply.

---

[10]Rob Feld, "In Praise of Confusion," *Written By* (December 2002–January 2003), reprinted in Charlie Kaufman, *Adaptation: The Shooting Script* (New York: Dey Street Books, 2002), 130.

Part II

GOODNESS

Four

LOOKING FOR GOODNESS

People seem to be attracted to evil. Dark, violent movies make lots of money. Actors often report that the most interesting roles to play are villains. Good characters seem to embody less complexity. Evil characters are more fun. Even in literature we see this trend. Many people think that in Milton's *Paradise Lost* Satan is a much more interesting character than the other angels or God. William Blake famously wrote, "The reason Milton wrote in fetters when he wrote of Angels & God, and at liberty when of Devils & Hell, is because he was a true Poet and of the Devil's party without knowing it."[1] The implication is that a true poet will have more sympathy with Satan than with any of the morally good characters. Although other literary critics dispute this claim, it is one with common currency.[2] There is something intriguing about evil, and we seem to be attracted to it.

---

[1]William Blake, *The Marriage of Heaven and Hell*, in *The Oxford Anthology of English Literature*, vol. 2, *1800 to the Present*, ed. Frank Kermode and John Hollander (New York: Oxford University Press, 1973), 36, plate 5.

[2]See Merritt Y. Hughes, introduction to John Milton, *Paradise Lost*, new ed. (New York: MacMillan, 1962), xix-xx, where Hughes writes, "It is only in the first two books of

But are we?

One night, shortly after I finished college, I was woken by pounding on my apartment door. I heard yelling. "Open up! Someone help me!" Startled into consciousness, I stumbled to the door. Standing there was a man holding his bare chest with a hand full of blood. I pulled him inside and laid him on the floor. "I was stabbed!" he barked out. I grabbed a towel to stop the blood. My roommate called the police while I put pressure on the wound. Fortunately, the knife hit his sternum and did not penetrate very far. It was his girlfriend. They had fought about a phone bill.

I was terrified. My neighbor turned out to be fine, but for the next week, I was in a daze. Violence is ugly. It disrupts all normal life patterns. How could a phone bill turn into this? It was nothing like TV. I like watching detective shows. I enjoy the intrigue. There is a challenge in figuring out the clues and an excitement that comes with closing in on the killer. I may feel a thrill watching the television story, but that thrill is nothing at all like seeing a stabbing firsthand. Television excitement is artificial. Real violence is sickening. I could not face what the real police face.

We seem to be attracted to evil, but mostly if it is fictional. It is the dramatic tension between good and evil that makes these kinds of stories compelling. We enter vicariously into the kinds of conflicts that would terrify us if we actually experienced them. From the safety of our homes, we can enjoy confrontations with terrible evil. We take up the vantage point of an observer at a safe distance. When it comes to our direct participation in reality, evil shakes us deeply. We strongly prefer goodness.

Paradise Lost that Satan seems heroic. There is grandeur but no heroism in his later soliloquies and after the seduction of Eve he departs to Hell, leaving the world to his vice-regents Sin and Death. There is no doubt of Milton's intent to degrade him, step by step, down to the scene of his second and involuntary appearance in serpent form in Book X."

Not only do we prefer what is good, but we want to *be* good. If you ever get a chance, listen to two people who are engaged in a moral disagreement. I do not mean a theoretical discussion, such as whether capitalism is inherently immoral. I mean a more concrete discussion. Listen to two people who are arguing about whether what one of them did was right or wrong. These discussions usually play out along the same story line. The person accused of doing wrong will take great pains to argue that his action was not wrong after all. Or he will insist that there were special circumstances that excused his behavior. You will hardly ever hear the story play out in the following way:

"What you did was wrong."
"Yes, but I really do not care about morality."
"Oh, I'm sorry, I thought you did."
"No, I'm not playing the moral game."
"I'm sorry. My mistake."

There are two things we can notice about these kinds of disagreements. First, we are anxious to show that we have acted rightly. We go to great pains to clear up misunderstandings about our behavior and our motives. In short, we want to be *seen* to be good. This desire might be a matter of hypocrisy. Sometimes, I suppose, it is. I think usually it is not. Hypocrisy is one thing we tend to judge harshly. So, although we do want to be known to be good, we want people to know that we are good because we *are* good. We want the reputation of being a person who does what is right, and we want our reputation to match the reality. The second thing to notice is that we want to show others that we have acted rightly. People in nearly every moral dispute agree that moral assessments apply to them. Whatever a true moral assessment amounts to, it sticks. It is not something we can evade just because we want to avoid it. No matter how deeply two people disagree about whether one of them was wrong, they agree that people should not act wrongly.

Early on I mentioned that each person has the project of navigating the world with a view to living well. We pursue this project with a sense of what makes for a good life. The flip side is that each of us has some idea of the kind of life we hope to avoid. Our set of preferences in this regard is mapped onto ideas about what is good and bad, and what is better and worse. We pursue what we think will be good, and we avoid those things that we deem bad. This pursuit aims to achieve both nonmoral and moral goods. A person navigates her life, in part, by her choices to become a certain kind of person. We want to be people who are morally good, people who embody the virtues and habits that we think are important and right. In short, we aim to become good people. We want to have the settled confidence that we are the kind of people we ought to be.

Every worldview or philosophy of life has to have both a story about goodness and a story about evil. That is, a worldview must include theories that make sense of these things. Goodness and evil represent some of the deep features of our experience of reality for which we want an account. Both in philosophical circles and throughout our culture it is more common to want an account of the existence of evil than to seek an account of goodness. We see this desire especially in discussions about belief in God. Such discussions are often framed in terms of whether the evil we encounter counts as strong evidence against the existence of a good God. I am not going to take up answering this question directly. I think the challenges that evil raises to the reasonability of believing in God are serious, but I also think that they can be successfully met. Because I am not defending the *truth* of the Christian picture of reality here, I will not develop a defense of this claim.[3] Instead, I am arguing that the

---

[3]I have explored the argument against God's existence based on evil in a number of places. For introductory treatments, see *Thinking About God: First Steps in Philosophy* (Downers Grove, IL: InterVarsity Press, 2004), 109-49, and "Evidential Problems of Evil," coauthored with Yena Lee, in *Evil: Christian Reflections on God and the Problem of Pain*, ed. Chad Meister, Norman Geisler, and James K. Dew Jr. (Downers Grove, IL: InterVarsity Press,

Christian story makes sense of our deepest grasp of how things are. Thus I shall explore goodness and investigate how it connects with alternative pictures of reality.

2013), 15-25. For a more detailed account, see "God and Evil," in *The Rationality of Theism*, ed. Paul Copan and Paul K. Moser (London: Routledge, 2003), 259-77.

Five

GOODNESS IS PRIMARY

One day my wife was driving my daughter and her friend to our house after school. Something happened, and the car just stopped. Jeanie managed to pull it off the parkway and called the tow truck. Our daughter and her friend sat by the side of the road and did their homework. For our daughter, this was a pretty common experience. Her friend, however, had never been in a car while it broke down. In fact, it was on her bucket list! She was thrilled with the experience. She could not wait to tell her parents!

Most of us have had bad cars. A car is bad because it does not do what it is supposed to do. It breaks down on the highway. To call our car bad is not to make a *moral* judgment. Things can be good or bad in a variety of ways. We have had a long series of bad cars, I have a bad shoulder, and I am a bad basketball player. These assessments do not involve moral categories. There are many ways of being bad besides being morally bad.

I know that I wade into turbulent waters when I begin to talk about the way we think of goodness or badness. The topic is especially tricky when we begin to talk about moral goodness and moral badness. Few areas invite more disagreement than the moral area. Yet we can make progress by recognizing that we disagree about morality primarily in two places. First, we disagree about the *content* of morality. That is, we often disagree about whether some particular action is right or wrong. We disagree, next, about our moral *theory*. Philosopher Robert Adams explains that moral theories concern the *nature* of morality.[1] Moral theories are, well, theoretical. They aim to answer questions such as: What is it that makes something right or wrong? What grounds moral truths? Given that it is a moral truth that, for example, we ought to be generous with others, what is it that makes this truth true? Answers to these questions are part of our worldview. Adams distinguishes our theories about morality from our *concepts* of morality. A person's concept of morality is captured by what she means when she uses moral terms such as *goodness* and *evil*. Here we find much agreement.

Let us think about our moral concepts. What are we *doing* when we call some action right or we call some person morally good? What are we recommending? When we call someone a good person, we are affirming his character. We approve of his actions. Furthermore, we are not merely indicating *our* approval. We are saying that he *ought* to be approved. Our moral judgment indicates that we want people and things to be good. And we think that they should be good.

When we call something bad we are expressing rejection. We aim to avoid or to change the situation. We want to stop things from being evil. Again, most people are not merely expressing their own preferences when they call an action evil. They take themselves to be ascribing something objectively true of the evil action. It is not merely that I dislike the way a person acts, but I take it that people ought not to act this way. When we call something evil, we are saying that there is something really wrong with it.

Despite the fact that there may be differences of opinion about whether a particular action is morally wrong and about the best theory of morality, we can see that our moral concepts are widely shared.

[1]See Robert M. Adams, "Divine Command Ethics Modified Again," in *The Virtue of Faith and Other Essays in Philosophical Theology* (New York: Oxford University Press, 1987), 128-43.

When we employ these evaluative terms, we mean generally the same things. There is not much danger of disagreement about what we mean, even if there are differences in the implications of what we mean. As a result, we can begin with this common ground, and we can explore how our notions of good and evil fit into various worldviews.

We admire people who exemplify what is good. Their stories inspire us, and we hope to emulate them. We want our relationships to flourish, and we want to achieve the things we value. The life we aim to live is a life that is good. In addition, we expect that we will be able to achieve these things. It becomes clear, as we reflect on these facts, that we are all drawn toward goodness.

Some years ago I was leading a discussion in a philosophy class on the problem of evil. We spent a couple of weeks discussing the challenges that various facts about evil pose for the existence of God. I noticed that as we talked about the severity of evil in the world the students became more and more despondent. I could see it in their body language. Their shoulders began to sag, and their chins drifted closer and closer to the table. There was an oppressive atmosphere in the room. On a whim I told the class that I would ask two questions and that I wanted each person to answer both. I asked, first, whether they thought there was more good than evil in the world, or whether there was more evil than good. Second, I asked whether they thought that most people think their lives are worth living. As each student answered, the consensus was very strong. It was not unanimous, but almost every one of them asserted that there was more good than evil in the world and that most people thought their lives were worth living. As they reported their answers, their posture changed. They perked up.

Do we think there is more good than evil in the world? A strong majority of my students thought so. Some people will say that students are naive. Others will say they are unduly cynical. One thing is clear: we tend to see the evil more clearly than we see the good. In fact, goodness is often invisible to us. We tend to see what we do not expect. If we expect something to be the case, then we do not pay attention to it. When I get into my car, I rarely notice when it starts. Fifteen or twenty times a week I turn the key, but I never think about it. I expect it to start, and it does. If it ever fails to do so, I am shocked. I pay attention. Something is wrong and needs to be fixed. Most weeks, however, I do not even think about the starter. Perhaps goodness is invisible because we expect it to be there. We expect the world to be good and our lives to be rewarding. It is only when something interferes with the goodness that we are startled into noticing. Evil is an intrusion into the normal. When something intrudes, we want to know why. When nothing intrudes, we do not ask questions about why things are the way they are. It is not until the normal is disturbed that we begin looking for explanations.

The expectation that things will be good makes it easy for us to forget that we ought to seek an account for the existence of goodness as well as for evil. That goodness often escapes our notice might explain why we seldom look for such an account. We operate as if goodness is the norm. We think that goodness is basic to reality. If we did not assume that reality is good in some sense, we would be more conscious of the need for an explanation for goodness when we encounter it.

Christianity makes sense of our expectations concerning goodness. This connection is made clear by reflecting on another observation about the Christian picture of reality: *In the Christian story, goodness is primary, and evil is a distortion.* If God exists, as noted above, God is the ultimate reality. Everything depends on God, and God is good. Everything depends on and is related to a fundamental good. Goodness is at the very center of reality.

God made the universe, and God made human beings for reasons, and these reasons are good. God's plans and intentions are for our good and for the good of the whole cosmos. God created a good world and gave us the capacities to cultivate it and enjoy it. Thus we are on solid ground when we expect that the universe will be a good place. The world is good. It has value intrinsically because it is the work of a good God.

Evil is a distortion. It is parasitic on this good. It is an intrusion that twists the original good features of reality. Because evil is a distortion, there can be no intrinsic evil as there can be intrinsic good.[2] Every case of evil is a corruption or distortion of some good thing. This picture of evil as a distortion of good makes sense of how we take up our moral stance in the world. We are against evil *because* we are for the good. We hate evil because we love the people and the things that evil destroys. We resist the distorting power of evil because we long to protect and preserve the good and beautiful things.

The picture that goodness is primary and that evil is a distortion fits with how we use our moral terms. The moral uses of *good* and *bad* are related to their nonmoral senses. A good car is one that runs reliably. It does what it is supposed to do. A good basketball player consistently accomplishes the goals of playing basketball according to the rules. A bad pencil sharpener fails to sharpen pencils. It does not accomplish its purpose. The moral assessments we make have similar structures. When we say that someone is a good person, we mean that she does good things and embodies good character. In other words, she acts as she ought to act, she loves what she ought to love, and she embodies the kinds of virtues and dispositions that a person in her circumstances ought to embody. When we call a situation or a person evil, we are making a related assessment. It is a situation that ought not to be. A person who does something evil fails to act as she ought, and she fails to embody the virtues she ought to embody. In fact, philosopher R. Douglas Geivett has articulated and defended the notion that the best characterization of evil is captured by the simple

---

[2]Augustine was the first major thinker to articulate this understanding explicitly. See for example *Enchiridion* 11-15.

assessment that "things ought not be this way."[3] A corollary to this characterization of evil is that goodness can be understood as the assessment that "this is the way things ought to be."

The characterization of goodness and of evil that Geivett articulated can be seen in some recent discussions between theists and atheists. Many atheists have argued that the influence of religion in the world has been mostly bad. They point to things such as slavery, cultural imperialism, and support for oppressive regimes. An example of this kind of argument is found in Christopher Hitchens's book *God Is Not Great: How Religion Poisons Everything*.[4] In contrast, most theists think that the overall influence of theistic belief has been good for human beings and for society. They will point to things such as literacy, hospitals, education, and the commitment to universal human rights. In this debate the disagreement centers on two issues. First, there is disagreement about the conclusion that is best supported by the historical evidence. What results have religious beliefs and practices actually produced? Second, there may be disagreement about the content of morality. Are the things that resulted from religious beliefs and practices morally wrong or not? There is no disagreement here about the *concept* of morality. Even Hitchens's subtitle is instructive. Religion is bad because, presumably, it poisons everything. It takes what is good and it twists it. Religion, he thinks, makes things the way they ought not be. Thus the way things ought to be is good, and goodness is primary.

This picture of good and evil reflects what Augustine thought about being a good person. As we saw previously, a good person loves good

[3]R. Douglas Geivett, "A Neglected Aspect of the Problem of Evil," unpublished paper presented at the national meeting of the American Academy of Religion, November 19, 1998. Another philosopher who articulates the characterization of evil along a similar line is Richard Gale. See his essay "Evil as Evidence Against God," in *Debating Christian Theism*, ed. J. P. Moreland, Chad Meister, and Khaldoun Sweis (Oxford: Oxford University Press, 2013), 197-207.

[4]Christopher Hitchens, *God Is Not Great: How Religion Poisons Everything* (New York: Twelve, 2007).

things in the right order. A person fails to be good when he loves things that are themselves good, but he loves them in the wrong order. Thus vice or evil in a person is a matter of disordered loves. Our loves ought to be ordered in a certain way. When our affections are captured to an inordinate degree by some lesser good, our loves become disordered. We prefer lesser goods at the expense of greater ones. I often prefer my own comfort to the needs of my family. I will choose to sit and read rather than get up and help Jeanie clean the house. What *I* want takes precedence over what Jeanie wants. This disorder is a state that reflects confusion or a disruption in the proper ordering of my loves. For Augustine, it is not that the disorder is some kind of force that works its way into our souls. We choose the order of our loves, and thus we choose this kind of disorder. Our loves are not ordered the way they ought to be ordered.

Again, we can see that goodness is the norm and evil is an intrusion. It is not simply that we believe that goodness is primary. We *feel* deeply that this is the way things are. It strikes us as right or fitting when things are good. We experience a settled contentment when we recognize the presence of goodness. We sense that this is the way the world ought to be.

For twenty years I lived in Connecticut. When spring finally arrived, I would take every opportunity to sit on our deck and read. The gentle breeze rustling the trees against the quiet of the neighborhood invited me to pause and to think. Reading gives way to reflection. Life is good. I recognize in a concrete way that my life is good, and I become filled with gratitude. These are moments of clarity and contentment. They are glimpses of the goodness that is present in my life and throughout the world. Deep down, we know that reality is good, that goodness is fundamental. From time to time, we can feel it to be the case.

The Christian story captures our expectations that goodness is primary and that evil is a distortion. If the atheistic story is true, as we have noted, the most fundamental reality is not personal. There is no value or goodness at the center. There can be no value until there are persons to ascribe such value. Thus, as far as reality is concerned, there is no reason to think that goodness should be primary. What is primary is without intrinsic value altogether. Goodness should startle us because we should not expect it.

Furthermore, in light of the atheistic commitment that the world is accidental, there is little reason to think that there is a way things ought to be. There can be a way we *want* things to be, but what this idea captures is our preferences. Our preferences do not ground objective purpose or value. A way things ought to be implies some kind of overarching purpose or goal. There can be no such purpose or goal unless there is someone to have the goal.

It is true that things can function well or function poorly without an overarching goal, but there cannot be a way things ought to be without one. So we can say that a plant is healthy or unhealthy in that its metabolic processes are functioning well or not. We cannot say that the plant *ought* to be healthy. In the atheistic story, the only purposes or goals are those created or chosen by some human being. Reality itself is devoid of independent or intrinsic purpose. Once persons arrive on the scene, we find that we have preferences about how we want reality to turn out. If we say that the plant ought to be healthy, we are imposing our own goals or desires on the plant. We are ascribing something to the plant that is not there. In an atheistic account, goodness as something real and foundational looks like an anomaly. It is not something we would expect.

The Christian story makes better sense of the fact that goodness is primary than the atheist picture of reality does. When a student asked me a few years ago if I could produce any reason to think that God is good, independent of the claims of any scriptures, I pointed out the deep assumption we share that goodness is primary and evil is a distortion. This conviction is widespread and persistent. If there is a God, it makes sense that God would have a nature that is the ground of all goodness. I mentioned that this fact is often invisible, but that we are convinced that it is the case. He had never considered this notion before, but he recognized this assumption, and it struck him as a good reason.

The Christian story is one in which we *find* value. We do not impose it or invent it. There is a way things ought to be because there is purpose. A good God created the universe for good reasons. Goodness is real. It is waiting for us, so to speak. We discover it in our encounter with the world. In order to recognize this feature of reality, we must pay attention because its pervasiveness renders it easy for us to overlook it.

Sometimes we stumble over goodness as if it is lying across our path. I was sixteen years old, and it had been about seven months since my family had moved from Maryland to central New Jersey. There were lots of transitions in my life. My sister, younger brother, and I were in a new school trying to find our way (my two older brothers were off at college). Although these situations can be terribly awkward for teenagers, we were finding life to be good. We connected quickly with many new friends. Our new school was a great environment for us.

Music had always been among the most important things in my life. I got hooked on the Beatles nearly from the beginning; Simon and Garfunkel in 1968; Crosby, Stills, Nash & Young in 1970. The combination of great tunes and meaningful lyrics shaped my whole approach to reality. My new friends and I quoted lyrics the way lawyers quote legal precedents: "Neil Young said it, I rest my case!" Right around my sixteenth birthday, much to my parents' dismay, I discovered Bob Dylan. This was 1972. Dylan had been recording for ten years already, so I was a little late in the game. Nonetheless, I was captured! At the same time, I was working hard at my own guitar playing and songwriting.

One day, I was struck hard with the thought: *There is too much goodness in the world for it to be an accident!* It was a flash of insight, all at once. My experience of friends, music, and life simply cried out for an explanation. The thought hit me that God had to be real. God had to be good, and God had to be close. I could find no other explanation for the goodness in my life and in the world. This was a turning point in my own story. My life direction began to change. Although this thought hit me all at once, I now see that this insight was grounded on my need to have an account of goodness. I had stumbled over goodness, and it pointed me to God. If God is real, it makes sense that reality is infused with goodness. It made sense to me then, and it makes sense to me still.

We have, I suggest, a deep expectation that things are and ought to be good. This expectation is seen in the myriad of things that makes our lives worth living to us. It is also seen in the very challenge that evil brings to our lives and to the question of the existence of God. That reality, at its core, is or ought to be good can also be recognized as we reflect on particular cases of evil. Whether we are talking about small frustrations such as the small choices we often make to be selfish or the breakdown of our cars, or about more serious challenges such as disease and systemic injustice, each case is a matter of something going wrong. The starter should turn the engine over. A disease disrupts the functioning of the human body. Economic or political systems that ought to balance power and protect the weak can be bent in order to serve the ends of oppression. Each time a person chooses to be selfish, there is something wrong with her moral orientation. She is not choosing as she ought. Her loves are disordered. Our engagement with the world reflects that we sense that evil is a distortion of what ought to be good. Thus, our experience of goodness and of evil fits well with the Christian picture of reality. The Christian story explains why the primacy of goodness strikes us as the way things are.

Six

GOODNESS IS GOOD FOR US

When I was working on my master's degree, I wrote a long paper on Augustine's theory of knowledge. It was thirty-eight pages! Now that I *grade* papers, I realize that it was too long. It is almost cruel to ask an instructor to grade that kind of paper. As soon as it was returned, I flipped to the back page to see my grade. I got an A! Then I noticed that every page of the paper was covered in red ink. There were *hundreds* of comments. My heart sank. Jeanie said to me, "You got an A. When are you going to be happy?" I replied, "When the only comment is, 'Publish this paper immediately.'"

What is wrong with me? I had enrolled in the MA program so that I could learn philosophy. There is no way to learn to do philosophy well without taking a lot of criticism. You *want* your professors to go over your writing with a fine-tooth comb. Every criticism helps you write more clearly. Although I am now grateful for the careful and thorough feedback, at the time it depressed me. I resisted. I wanted to be a good philosopher, but I did not want to go through what it takes to *become* a good philosopher. Criticism, even criticism that I know is good for me, is difficult to accept. I always squirm under it.

One summer I drove from my parents' home in New Jersey to where I was working in Minnesota. Somewhere in Indiana, I saw the all-too-familiar flashing lights of a state trooper. I was speeding, and I knew it. I was going sixty-eight in a fifty-five zone. Again, I had a pit in my stomach. I hated the fact that I was caught. Not only does a speeding ticket cost money, but my ego took a hit as well. I was resentful. I don't like being in the wrong. More than that, I hate being held accountable when I am wrong!

Earlier I claimed that we are attracted to goodness and that we think that moral assessments apply to us. Something happens, however, when someone *else* applies an assessment to me. I duck and weave like a boxer. I find that even if the criticism is not a moral one, I resist. So, despite the fact that I want to be a good philosopher and a good driver and, even more so, a good person, I react with evasion and excuses when someone suggests how I might be better. What I resist, I think, is being forced to admit that I am not what I ought to be. Not only am I not what I ought to be, but the other person *knows* I am not what I ought to be. Being criticized or challenged brings both embarrassment and disappointment with myself. Although I want to be good, I want to be good *already*. I do not want to have to work at becoming good. I want people to recognize that I am good. I do not want them to recognize that I fall short.

I do think we are attracted to goodness, but the story is more complicated. We are motivated to be good, but we resist being under scrutiny. We want to pass with high grades, but often we do not want to take the test. Moral assessments, in particular, are difficult to undergo. Yet our culture is increasingly filled with moral judgments. A friend of mine once commented that, despite the fact that many people claim to be relativists about morality, our culture is more moralistic than ever. Moral responsibility permeates nearly every feature of our lives, and no one has asked why. That is, no one asked until

Friedrich Nietzsche came along. He asked unprecedented and profound questions about our practices of making moral judgments:

> Under what conditions did man invent the value judgments of good and evil? *And what value do they themselves have?* Have they up to now obstructed or promoted human flourishing? Are they a sign of distress, poverty and the degeneration of life? Or, on the contrary, do they reveal the fullness, vitality and will of life, its courage, its confidence, its future?[1]

Although we think consciously about the *content* of our moral evaluations, that we make such judgments is taken for granted. We hardly notice. Nietzsche wants to press us to think about the fact that we make value judgments. He wants us to consider these practices in a new light. So he poses the questions: Where did our practices of making moral judgments come from? What good are they?

The way Nietzsche frames his questions reveals what he thinks is most important. For Nietzsche, the justification of our moral practices is grounded solely in whether they promote flourishing. Do these practices contribute to human well-being or not? A further question is, if our moral practices contribute to our flourishing, why do I resist them?

Nietzsche has his own story to tell about both the origin and the value of traditional moral practice. He argues that the human practice of making moral judgments was born out of resentment. Human communities have always consisted of strong and powerful people as well as weak and powerless people. The strong tend to exploit and oppress the weak. This exploitation produces resentment. Nietzsche's view is that moral judgment began as the weak people attempted to exact revenge. They wanted to exercise control over the strong. Since

[1]Friedrich Nietzsche, *On the Genealogy of Morality*, ed. Keith Ansell-Pearson, trans. Carol Diethe, Cambridge Texts in the History of Political Thought (Cambridge: Cambridge University Press, 1994), preface, section 3. Italics original.

the weak could not overcome the strong directly, they did so indirectly. They labeled all of the features that characterize the strong "evil." Thus the exercise of power and the use of other people for one's own purposes came to be thought of as morally bad. Then they took all of their own qualities, such as weakness, timidity, and cowardice, and elevated them into virtues. Nietzsche calls this strategy the "revaluation of all values."[2] He describes how the deficient character qualities of the weak are inverted to become moral values:

> Lies are turning weakness into an *accomplishment*, no doubt about it . . . and impotence which doesn't retaliate is being turned into "goodness"; timid baseness is being turned into "humility"; submission to people one hates is being turned into "obedience." . . . Not-being-able-to-take-revenge is called not-wanting-to-take-revenge, it might even be forgiveness.[3]

The qualities we think of as virtues are really resentments turned upside down. Rather than actually achieving power, the weak simply turned values over in order to preserve their dignity in the face of oppression. The startling thing, for Nietzsche, is that this strategy worked.

One conclusion Nietzsche draws is that since the origin of moral judgments is found in a strategy to channel resentment, there is no reason to suppose these judgments ascribe anything real or true to the persons being evaluated. The practice of making moral judgments, then, does not track truth about reality. He thus argues that moral truths, in the way they have been traditionally understood, do not exist. There are only resentments and strategies to act them out.

A second conclusion Nietzsche defends is that not only are these practices suspect in their origin, but they are also currently among the most severe enemies of life. Have the practices of making moral judgments "up to now obstructed or promoted human flourishing?"

[2]Ibid., 1.7.
[3]Ibid., 1.14. Italics original.

Nietzsche claims that they block the pursuit of the best human life. To explain how these practices hinder flourishing, Nietzsche introduces what he calls the *ascetic ideal.* The ascetic ideal can be found in any claim that we are obligated to submit our passions and drives to some higher goal or calling. Its roots go as far back as Plato, who argued that the morally ordered person is the one in whom the rational part of the soul controls the spirited and appetitive parts.[4] Christian views of moral reality also embody the ascetic ideal, because we are to refrain from exerting our self-will and embrace the call to love others as we love ourselves. Nietzsche rejected any version of the ascetic ideal. Each version requires us to turn away from the very things that make up life and to enter into bondage. We sacrifice our drives, passions, and desires to the higher calling, and thus we trade life for death. The moral posture, then, is bad for us.

If we are honest with ourselves, we will admit that Nietzsche's view resonates with our resistance to moral assessment. As I mentioned at the opening of this chapter, I often experience this desire to be free from interference. I feel squelched by another person's negative judgment on my behavior or my character. If Nietzsche is correct, this resistance is among our deepest desires. At the level of our core identities, what we want is to have nothing interfere with the expression of our drives to exert ourselves or to fulfill our own passions. He urges us to live our lives under aesthetic categories rather than under moral ones. Our lives should be artistic creations expressing beauty, joy, and passion. Moral categories, such as duty or obligation, impose limits on our self-expression.

Nietzsche's assessment is original and thought provoking, but we can challenge the claim that our moral practices hinder our flourishing. The truth of the matter depends on how flourishing should be understood. We can compare the vision of flourishing in Nietzsche's

---

[4]See Plato, *Republic* 435a-445e.

view with that in the Christian view to see which resonates best with our deeper assumptions about what is good in life.

Nietzsche thinks that following the Christian or any other traditional moral view involves turning away from those things that make our lives worth living and subsuming them under some external standard or ideal. Thus we reject the very things that we want most in life because we feel forced to pursue some other goal that does not capture what we most deeply want. So, let us address some questions head-on. What is it that we actually want most in life? What do we think we *should* want? What kind of persons do we want to be? What sort of relationships do we want to experience with those around us?

When most of us reflect on our lives, we recognize that our deepest desires are more complicated than simply the desire to resist assessment. Most deeply, we want our lives to be filled with relationships characterized by trust, love, encouragement, and genuine concern. It is impossible to experience these kinds of relationships unless we discipline our drive to exert our own will. It is clear that if we give free rein to what Nietzsche calls the "will to power" we cannot have the kinds of relationships we most want. I must point out that, as far as I can tell, Nietzsche never recommends that individuals indulge their will to power in their interpersonal relations. Rather, he explicitly argues that all of our endeavors are, at bottom, driven by competing drives to power. Flourishing requires that we order our drives in the way that appeals to us most. We do not order our drives on the basis of traditional morality. We act for aesthetic reasons. I am my own canvas, and I paint my life how I want. There are no rules about how I ought to do so.

In sharp contrast to Nietzsche's views stands the Christian story. The value of our moral practices for human life can be captured in the next observation: *In the Christian story, goodness is good for us.* The life that embodies moral virtue is the best life. Following moral reality promotes rather than hinders human flourishing. As we saw in earlier chapters, Christianity tells us that God created human beings for conscious reasons. This fact grounds the objective meaning of our lives. Since God is good (and the divine nature is the standard of goodness), the reasons and the goals for creating are likewise good. God made human beings, in part, so we can experience goodness by embodying virtues that reflect God's own goodness. Thus God's plan for us tracks moral reality, since both moral reality and God's design for us come from the same source: the divine nature.

A Christian view of the moral life makes sense of the fact that the morally good life is the best life to live. The virtues of generosity, humility, love, and forgiveness are not euphemisms for weakness and failure, as Nietzsche claimed. They turn out to be the path to the richest relationships. Rather than reflecting an impoverished life, they reflect life in all of its fullness. What I want most for my life is found in the very view put forward by Christianity. Furthermore, the kind of practices that a Christian perspective would label as bad or evil are the very things that undermine the possibility of the quality of relationships for which we long. The connection between the content of a Christian morality and the virtues that contribute to a better life is not accidental. God designed us to embody these virtues. Doing so is part of the well-functioning life. When you treat another person with kindness and respect, she feels known and accepted. She is able, then, to respond with understanding. Your relationship becomes deeper as you embody these relational virtues.

If human flourishing is at least in part a matter of entering and experiencing relationships characterized by qualities of love, trust, and loyalty, then Nietzsche is mistaken in his claim that traditional moral practices hinder human flourishing. The practices that encourage our relationships to flourish are the practices that promote our well-being. These practices are the very ones that make up the moral life. There is a stunning fact here: The morally good life is the humanly good life.

To be sure, Nietzsche's conclusions about morality do not make up the only atheist view about the origin and value of the practice of making moral judgments. As we noted earlier, many contemporary atheists believe that the origin of our moral practices, like our relational practices and religious practices, can be explained by the story of unguided Darwinian evolution.[5] Rather than having risen out of resentment, our moral practices arose out of the struggle to survive. There are lots of variations among the Darwinian explanations of our moral practices. Some theorists think that they developed as a result of group selection. Another theory is that they emerged as a byproduct of other features that had survival value. What all of these theories have in common is the notion that our current moral practices originated in primitive habits that directly or indirectly gave those who engaged in them an edge in survival and reproduction.

Behavior that led to self-sacrifice and cooperation helped the communities that practiced them work together more effectively. As a result, communities whose individuals felt the pull toward cooperation and self-sacrifice survived better than other communities. The tendency to feel that we are obligated to embody self-sacrifice and cooperation spread throughout the population. In this kind of Darwinian story, the sense that we had these moral obligations did help us survive. In this way, moral practices helped the human community flourish.

We can see, then, that Darwinian theories, regardless of whether they are guided or unguided, have the resources to explain the origin of practices that contribute to our flourishing. On these views, the well-being for the individual is a byproduct of the well-being of the community. We noticed before that in the Christian story our flourishing is also closely connected to our relationships within the community. Although Darwinian stories are often summarized with the quip "survival of the fittest," it would be a mischaracterization of these

---

[5]See Daniel Dennett, *Breaking the Spell: Religion as a Natural Phenomenon* (New York: Viking, 2006), chaps. 6-7.

theories to think that this slogan captures the *content* of the kind of morality that best fits with Darwinism. Instead, we are hardwired for behavior that leads to our well-being.

There are two aspects of these Darwinian stories that should give us pause. First, although it is a fact that cooperation and self-sacrifice contribute to relational flourishing, the Darwinian stories cannot explain why we are *obligated* to follow these practices. It is the *feeling* that we have these moral obligations and not the existence of *real* obligations that had survival value. The Darwinian story can tell us how human beings came to be the kinds of creatures that feel these obligations. It tells us nothing about whether there are real obligations that are binding on us. We can see that flourishing is good. But on unguided Darwinian stories, this good is local. It is not a cosmic good. There is no grounding for our deep sense that we have obligations to contribute to the flourishing of others. On theistic views (including *guided* Darwinian stories), there is both local and global grounding for our obligations. There is a cosmic person to whom we are obligated in our dealings with one another.

The second concern with unguided Darwinian stories of morality concerns survival. Suppose we accept that moral feelings did help us survive in this way, but there are no objective moral obligations. What do we do now? The species has survived well already. A few years ago, the human population was reported to have reached seven billion people! Whether or not you and I continue to obey our moral feelings will make no difference to the future of the species. These feelings, then, are merely leftover debris of the unguided Darwinian process. Of course, it might not be possible to set aside our moral intuitions. After all, our moral impulses are deeply ingrained. We can see, however, that there is a tension between the unguided Darwinian stories about morality on the one hand and our convictions about the nature of morality on the other.

We recognize that there is goodness and that it is good for us. We are attracted to it. We also have a deep resistance to moral judgment and correction. We have strategies to evade and subvert moral assessments. We are conflicted about morality. Thus both the Christian story and Nietzsche's views initially seem to be plausible. They each reflect our experience. Discerning which captures our deeper desires, however, is not difficult. Ultimately we want what the Christian picture of reality offers. We want to experience and embody goodness.

Not only do we have these desires, but we feel deeply that we have obligations to act according to them. It would be a strange thing if our obligation to embody the virtues and practices that lead to the very kind of life we long to live were only imaginary. Once we see that the moral life is the good life, not just in the past as far as survival is concerned, but *now* in our present experience, we experience a strong dissonance between the unguided Darwinian story of morality or Nietzsche's views of value judgments, on the one hand, and the contours of our core identities, on the other.

The undeniable fact is that reality is infused with goodness, and goodness is good for us. Goodness is vital to our well-being. We long to become good people, and we aim to achieve good things. We celebrate goodness and we resist evil because it corrupts and destroys what is good. We are attracted to goodness as the needle of a compass points north. We have the deep hunch that this orientation toward goodness tracks with reality. The morally good life is the humanly good life. The Christian story lines up with what we most want. The world is shot through with value. It fits with what we know to be true and what we want to be true.

Part III

BEAUTY

Seven

THE STARTLING PRESENCE OF BEAUTY

In 1983 I spent the summer in the Philippines working with college students. Our small team, made up of Americans and Filipinos, was based in the city of Iloilo in Western Visayas. One weekend we took some R&R on a small, remote island. It took about half a day to reach our destination. We traveled through small jungle islands on Jeepneys so packed with villagers that we had to climb on the roof or hang onto the sides. We crossed between islands in motorized outriggers. Our Filipino teammates told us that the children we met along the way had probably never seen a person of European descent.

As we crossed one of the straits, I stood up and clung to the small roof of the outrigger. The magnificence of the world stunned me. In one direction, smooth, clear water stretched to the horizon. In the other, small islands were scattered about, covered in palm trees and jungle growth. The fragrant breeze blew steadily in my face, filling my lungs with joy. I relished this feast. After some minutes, I began to reflect on the experience itself. It was a gift. It was a moment of beauty, and I simply received it. It was not a means *to* something else. I accepted it as it was. I wanted nothing from it.

Beauty presents itself to us. We do not look *for* beauty as if it were a static thing waiting to be found. Beauty encounters us. It is the beautiful that initiates, that moves, that captures our attention. We do not make the first step. Beauty, in some sense, seeks us. We may put ourselves in places that leave us open to beauty, but it is the beautiful that acts on us. In this dance, beauty leads. Literary theorist Elaine Scarry comments:

> Not Homer alone, but Plato, Aquinas, Plotinus, Pseudo-Dionysius, Dante, and many others repeatedly describe beauty as a "greeting." At the moment one comes into the presence of something beautiful, it greets you. It lifts away from the neutral background as though coming forward to welcome you—as though the object were designed to "fit" your perception.[1]

The notion of beauty as a greeting is packed full of insight. It suggests that beauty meets us in a manner unlike almost anything else in the world. Beauty startles us. It stops us in our tracks. It moves us to change directions. We do not glance at beautiful things or skim beautiful verses. To glance or to skim is to hold an object or text at a distance. And to hold something at a distance is to fail to encounter it. When it comes to beauty, to glance is to fail to see. Roger Scruton comments on the nature of beauty's call: "Beauty can be consoling, disturbing, sacred, profane; it can be exhilarating, appealing, inspiring, chilling. It can affect us in an unlimited variety of ways. Yet it is never viewed with indifference: beauty demands to be noticed; it speaks to us directly like the voice of an intimate friend."[2] Beauty greets us, then.

---

[1]Elaine Scarry, *On Beauty and Being Just* (Princeton, NJ: Princeton University Press, 1999), 25.

[2]Roger Scruton, *Beauty: A Very Short Introduction* (Oxford: Oxford University Press, 2011), xi.

But we might not hear it. We might not respond. It may be that we do not even recognize it.

Not long ago, Jeanie and I were hiking in Yosemite with some dear friends, Tony and Katie. Tony is a biological consultant and teaches environmental studies. Hiking with Tony is like getting your own behind-the-scenes tour. Each flower we encountered became the starting point of a rich discussion of the ecosystem. We saw the devastation the bark beetles brought to the Ponderosa pines, while the cedars were left untouched. Every question we asked opened many lines of inquiry. If we had hiked by ourselves, we would have skimmed the terrain and glanced at the flowers and birds. With Tony, we *saw* them. It sometimes takes an expert to see well.

Exploring a museum with an art historian would reveal more than I could ever see on my own. In one sense I would see the same paintings if I went by myself. I could count them, and maybe I could remember which artist produced which painting. The art historian would help me to see the painting *well.* She would reveal more than facts. She would reveal the beauty that would otherwise be invisible to me. I cannot see what the art historian sees. I do not have what it takes. Notice that when I fail to see what she sees, it is not merely a matter of us having different opinions about the painting. It is not simply that we disagree. I *fail* to see what is really there to be seen. The difficulty is not with the painting, with the art historian, or with our different perspectives. The difficulty is all mine. There is something missing in my ability to see. It is as if I were colorblind or tone-deaf. Beauty is there, but I do not have the eyes to see it.

This realization reminds me that beauty is as much a part of reality as things more easily seen. The color and the shape of an object are not more real than its beauty. They are just visible to more people. These features may be closer to the surface, but they are not more real. Beauty, like goodness, is a part of reality. But it is a part of reality that can be missed. Beauty calls to us, and we must pause to hear it. If we do not pause, we will miss it altogether. What is it to miss beauty? To miss beauty is to miss something fundamentally important to human life.

Philosophers have long commented on the connection between beauty, goodness, and truth. Inspired by Plato, Aristotle, and Plotinus, medieval thinkers, both Christian and Islamic, called beauty, goodness, and truth the *transcendentals.* The transcendentals are thought to lie behind all being. They are rooted in the being of God. As such they ground reality and are in some sense more deeply real than the things that reflect them. Roger Scruton contends, "Beauty is therefore as firmly rooted in the scheme of things as goodness. It speaks to us, as virtue speaks to us, of human fulfillment: not of things that we want, but of things that we ought to want, because human nature requires them."[3]

If these thinkers are correct, then beauty, as well as goodness and truth, is a nonnegotiable aspect of human life. It is woven deeply into the fabric of our humanity. The place of beauty in reality shapes the way we engage our world. Our own experiences concur with the idea that beauty is real and that it fits with how things ought to be. Beauty beckons to us.

[3]Ibid., 123.

Eight

THE ARTIST

When I worked at Yale, I would often walk through Phelps Gate to get onto campus. Under the arch was the door to the classics department. For a while, there was a sign on the door: "Annoy your parents. Major in Classics!" I loved it! Some academic pursuits simply do not seem practical. As a philosopher, I have had my share of questions about my course of study. Why would anyone be a philosopher? It seems so . . . odd! What will you *do* with a philosophy degree? Behind these questions there often lies an assumption about what is important or what counts as real. In the *real* world—the emphasis is always on *real*—classics or philosophy finds little place. This view of what is real or what is important is part of a larger critique of the humanities and the arts. We hear this larger critique whenever business leaders accuse universities of failing to prepare students for the work of business. What is the good of such study? These fields do not prepare students for the real world—that is, the business world. While philosophers may be dismissive of the concerns of business leaders, there are serious issues at stake. Is there actually a place for beauty in the real world?

I recall attending a panel discussion on the humanities. During interaction with the audience, one student referred to a recent scientific advance that had good hopes of reversing some kinds of blindness. She asked the question: "Given that we could be working to help blind people see, why should we consider investing our lives in the humanities?" One professor on the panel, without missing a beat, took the microphone and said, "Because we want there to be something worth seeing." The creation and contemplation of beauty complements rather than competes with the pursuit of more practical achievements. Both have value. If there were not things worth seeing, there would be little motivation to cure blindness.

There is a current of thought that the pursuit of beauty and other things, such as learning, belong to what we might call *high culture*, and therefore they are luxuries. Such pursuits are available only to the privileged few who have the leisure and resources to enjoy them. As a result, the pursuit of beauty is challenged on ethical grounds. First, preoccupation with beauty is thought to distract us from more important issues that require addressing. Second, high culture strikes many people as elitist. Only the rich and the educated can participate. A third charge against the value of beauty is that attention to the beauty of a person or thing is intrinsically exploitive. It is an attempt to use the object of perception for one's own purposes. It is, to use Immanuel Kant's ethical terms, to treat the beautiful person merely as a means and not also as an end.[1] What can we say about these charges?

It is true that the way our culture trades in beauty can be deeply exploitive. We see this reality in our fixation with the stars of television and film. Magazines regularly produce lists of the most beautiful women or men alive. Everyone on the list is a star. Beauty is reduced to a combination of fame, power, and overt sexuality. These magazines line the checkout aisle of supermarkets, tempting ordinary people to ascribe an extraordinary kind of life to the celebrities. Writer Walker Percy often observed that we perceive an almost divine kind

[1]For Kant's use of this terminology, see Immanuel Kant, *Groundwork of the Metaphysics of Morals*, ed. Mary Gregor (Cambridge: Cambridge University Press, 1997), 38.

of reality in movie stars, and at the same time we think ourselves barely real at all.[2]

Our appreciation of beauty is twisted as well by the advertising industry. When my daughter, Lizzy, was fourteen, I realized that there were people who were paid a lot of money to manipulate how she thought about love, sex, beauty, goodness, and what makes life worth living. All they wanted was for her to spend her money. These people did not care about *her*. They didn't care about what kind of person she was or about who she should be. They were paid to mold what she *wanted* to be. They aimed to control her dreams and desires in order to sell clothes, makeup, or some vision of life. Thus beauty and goodness and truth are bent into tools for sales.

The most pernicious expression of the exploitive manipulation of beauty is found in pornography. Human sexuality is quarantined from relationship and turned into a commodity. Sex is sold, isolated from any relation between persons as persons. Years ago I had a long discussion in which I could not convince a student that pornography is damaging to the men who watch it. (It is mostly men, after all.) I argued that watching pornography develops deep habits of viewing others as objects whose purpose is to satisfy our own needs. These habits corrode our ability to have relationships characterized by love and respect. He just could not see it. A couple of months later, I bumped into him on the street. He brought up the topic again: "You are right," he said, "pornography is destructive." I don't know whether he learned this from his own painful experience or had simply thought more deeply about it. Our relation to beauty, then, can be exploitive. Beauty is often distorted for other ends. This twisting is a violation of the nature of beauty as an end in itself.

The charge of elitism also has a ring of truth. The ability of some people to devote their careers to the artistic or literary or scholarly

---

[2]See Walker Percy, *Lost in the Cosmos: The Last Self-Help Book* (New York: Farrar, Straus and Giroux, 1983), 37-40.

enterprise is a luxury of an affluent society. In earlier centuries painters and writers either had other means of income or were sponsored by individuals, courts, or the church. There is, then, a luxury in being free to devote one's time to the artistic enterprise. Our drive to make and to enjoy the things of beauty, however, is deep and persistent. It is part of what it means to be human. What we produce or contribute to the world matters to us. We take pleasure and joy in the works of our hands. C. S. Lewis, who was both a literary critic and an author in his own right, explained this fact in an address he gave at the dawn of the Second World War. He reflected on the question of the value of culture making in times of great trouble:

> If men had postponed the search for knowledge and beauty until they were secure, the search would never have begun. . . . Plausible reasons have never been lacking for putting off all merely cultural activities until some imminent danger has been averted or some crying injustice put right. But humanity long ago chose to neglect those plausible reasons. They wanted knowledge and beauty now, and would not wait for the suitable moment that never comes.[3]

Elaine Scarry's work *On Beauty and Being Just* is a sustained argument against both the charge that pursuing beauty distracts us from our ethical and social obligations and the charge that it exploits the people and things we think are beautiful. Rather than distracting us from the concrete needs in the world or being exploitive, she argues that beauty "prepares us for justice."[4] The person who is responsive to beauty is in part practicing a sound and sane human life. She is more attuned to goodness and justice.

---

[3]C. S. Lewis, "Learning in War-Time," in *The Weight of Glory and Other Addresses* (New York: Macmillan, 1949), 44-45. The address was delivered in autumn 1939.

[4]Elaine Scarry, *On Beauty and Being Just* (Princeton, NJ: Princeton University Press, 1999), 78.

The fact is not that we are distracted by beauty but that we are too distracted or preoccupied to encounter it deeply. The competition for each person's attention is fierce, and we have only a finite amount of attention to give. We have even invented strategies, such as multitasking, to convince ourselves that we can accomplish more by dividing our finite attention into smaller and smaller bits. This practice is fitting for inhabitants of the information age. It is intriguing that our era has *not* been called the age of beauty or the age of wisdom or the age of contemplation. It is the age of information. Information demands from us only superficial attention.

Consider what it takes to excel in the information age. The age of information requires certain skills, and the practice of these skills habituates us into patterns of being, doing, and thinking that can strongly influence the kind of person we become. These skills are very different from those that would be required in an age of beauty or an age of wisdom. For example, information is an item that is to be assimilated, managed, and mastered. Beauty, in contrast, cannot be mastered. Beauty requires that we remain open, that we contemplate, that we order our lives around something outside our control. Information management requires speed; beauty demands slow, careful reflection. Information is always a means to some end. Beauty, in contrast, is an end in itself. We seek it for its own sake. Succeeding in the information age will make us less able to stop and hear beauty's call. Thus we treat beauty only superficially if at all. We dabble in it, but we do not allow it to touch us deeply. We make it into a commodity, and we become merely buyers and sellers. We participate in the manipulation of beauty.

Real beauty, however, lies buried like a cache of jewels. It is invisible to many, but it is there, waiting to be dug out and exhibited to the world. Those convinced of this claim order their steps accordingly.

Beauty calls to us, and it offers to reshape the contours of our lives according to its own rhythm. Years ago I was driving with my family through the redwood forest in Northern California. We pulled over at a random spot and hiked for an hour or so. We were completely alone. What struck us was the interplay of stillness and hugeness. The silence poured down from vast heights. The massive reach of the trees spoke of age, wisdom, and peace. We were in a wholly different time and place. We felt an invitation to breathe deeply, walk slowly, and rest in quiet. Beauty has its rhythm.

The majesty of beauty and its place in human flourishing fit well into the story Christianity holds forth. Thus we can articulate another observation: *In the Christian story, the most fundamental reality is a Master Artist.* Previously we explored the observations that, in the Christian story, the most fundamental reality is personal and intrinsically relational. We saw that these claims have significant implications for who we are and how we navigate the world. In the Christian story God creates everything that exists. When we talk about God's creating, we often use engineering language. Thus we speak of intelligence, fine-tuning, or design when we think about the initial conditions of the universe. All of this is perfectly appropriate. God *is* an engineer, and the universe is intricately designed for its particular purposes. As a result, it is knowable, complex, and suited for exploration. It is fit for human life and flourishing.

God is also an artist. Thus the universe is extraordinarily beautiful. The role of engineer may seem to conflict with the role of artist. My father, who was an aerospace engineer, explained that there was constant pressure to make things smaller, lighter, stronger, and cheaper. The engineer aims at functionality and efficiency. In a satellite, every pound matters. So the engineer works between the constraints set by the purpose of the satellite and the limitations of size, weight, energy, and the strength of various materials. Aesthetic qualities are secondary. There is, to be sure, something beautiful about a well-constructed satellite in geosynchronous orbit (about 36,000 kilometers from the surface of the earth). An artist, however, works differently from an engineer. There are fewer constraints on how to achieve the end goal.

The artist does not have to walk as narrow a line between function and materials. There are some constraints, but there is more freedom for personal expression in the creative process.

Unlike human engineers and artists, God's creative process is not constrained by any lack of resources. God has all of the resources imaginable to accomplish the purposes of creation. God as engineer grounds the efficacy of the design of the universe and everything in it. God as artist infuses it with striking beauty. Each of these aspects of God's creative nature is compelling. Many years ago, I was in an ongoing dialogue with an architect who at the time was not a Christian. In the course of one of our discussions, I raised this question: "Doesn't it make more sense that the universe is the product of an artist than that it is an accident?" Ben was an architect largely because he was an artist. He loved the study and creation of beauty. We had had numerous discussions about the history of architecture, the architecture at Yale in particular, and the role of beauty in design. His appreciation for beauty, and for the role of beauty in human flourishing, was deep, and he had shaped his life's work around the value of experiencing and creating beauty. His love of beauty resonated with the possibility of a cosmic artist. Something deep within the human soul resonates with beauty wherever it is found. Natural beauty haunts us, and we strive to create our own beauty through our buildings, public spaces, paintings, music, poetry, and a host of other expressions.

The Christian story is the story of a master artist. God made the universe not as a factory worker stamps out trinkets but as the sculptor creates in the studio or a composer works at the piano. God's purposes are broader than the practical concerns involved in providing an arena for knowledge and action. God's purposes are broader even than the moral goals of having us embody virtue. God's purposes involve the beautiful. After each day in the Genesis account of creation, the text reports: "And God saw that it was good" (Gen 1:4 ["And God saw that the light was good"]; Gen 1:10, 12, 18, 21, 25). At the end of this creation account, the text reads: "God saw everything that he had made, and indeed, it was very good" (Gen 1:31).

We get the sense that God takes great delight in the beauty of the world. There is an extravagant generosity to God's creation. The world points to overflowing joy. God's abundant giving in creation explains why there are so many galaxies and so many different kinds of frogs. Only a God who loves beauty would make so many!

Some years ago I was a guest lecturer in a philosophy class at the University of New Hampshire. My lecture covered some new works defending atheism. We had quite a good discussion. As the time drew to its end, the professor stepped in. "My question," he said, "is, why dinosaurs?" I think he wanted an account of why God would create dinosaurs when no human being would ever see them. I paused for a moment and replied, "Because they are so cool!" He laughed and thought it was a good answer. Why dinosaurs? Well, why not? Every eight-year-old boy knows that dinosaurs are amazing. God too knows this truth, and God creates amazing things with extravagant generosity.

It is no wonder the psalmist declares:

> The heavens are telling the glory of God;
> and the firmament proclaims his handiwork.
> Day to day pours forth speech,
> and night to night declares knowledge.
> There is no speech, nor are there words;
> their voice is not heard;
> yet their voice goes out through all the earth,
> and their words to the end of the world. (Ps 19:1-4)

The heavens overflow with the expression of the beauty of God. This poem suggests that, although they have no actual voice, they speak loudly. The beauty of God rings throughout the universe. Day and night there is the bubbling up of the unmistakable declaration of goodness and beauty. If Christianity is true, the universe *was* made by a cosmic artist. Reality is beautiful. Beauty is real. It leaks through every seam in the fabric of the cosmos! There is a true extravagance to the beauty we encounter.

God is the Master Artist not only in the sense of being the original or the supreme artist but also in that God's creativity is the source of all creativity. God not only makes art; God makes artists. God does not only make those who encounter beauty; God makes those who create beauty. God is a master in the way that there was a master in a medieval guild. God apprentices creatures to become artists. The human artistic drive, then, makes sense. We are artists, and our celebration of beauty has deep cosmic value because God is an artist. We are creative because God is the Creator. God's creativity extends throughout the universe. We are captured by beauty both as observers and as participants. When we create, we are imitating God. Art is profoundly human because it has a divine origin. Our artistic impulses reflect divine creativity. That God is an artist and a maker of artists makes sense of this piece of reality.

In the story of God's creation, human beings were given a task. We were to "be fruitful and multiply, and fill the earth and subdue it; and have dominion over the fish of the sea and over the birds of the air and over every living thing that moves upon the earth" (Gen 1:28). This task has been called the *cultural mandate*. It is the mandate to cultivate the world God has created and to bring forth fruitful things. That is, we have a mandate to make culture. In a sense God's act of creation is not complete. God invites us into the ongoing creation task. We are to shape what God has made and so bring out of it things that are good, useful, true, and beautiful. Theologian John Navone remarks on this notion: "Inasmuch as creation stands unfinished, God continues to call us from chaos to cosmos, from formlessness to the resplendent form of God's true images."[5] Our capacities to act freely and

---

[5]John Navone, SJ, *Toward a Theology of Beauty* (Collegeville, MN: Liturgical, 1996), 45.

efficaciously in the world reflect God's capacities to act freely and efficaciously. God brings forth a beautiful world and turns us loose to bring forth beautiful things within it. God is like the father of small children at a McDonald's restaurant with a huge playground. He holds their hands and leads them to the edge of the ball pit. Releasing their hands, he says, "Go explore!" God releases us into a glorious world to learn, celebrate, and enjoy! This is our humanity.

The point of the cultural mandate is not mere survival. The point is to make life delightful. We want there to be things worth seeing. The point is our flourishing and the flourishing of the whole created order. We are culture builders. We saw that John Stuart Mill claimed that it is our distinctly human capacities that make it possible for us to experience the richest life. The capacities he had in mind were largely the culture-making capacities—our capacities to produce and enjoy beauty.

Like everything good in human life, beauty is also fragile. We live in a fractured world. The Christian story includes a darker side. Due to human rebellion against God, our desires and capacities are distorted. We still produce beauty, but we participate in ugliness and evil as well. At the New York World's Fair in 1965, my family and I saw Michelangelo's *Pietà*. Even as an eight-year-old who was more interested in the dinosaurs at the Sinclair exhibit, I was amazed. The rich color of the marble, the tenderness of the expression on the face of Mary, and the sorrow of the scene captured me, even in my juvenile impatience. Over fifty years later, the memory stands out. The contemporary story of the *Pietà* took a darker turn. In 1972 an insane geologist smashed the sculpture with a hammer. Because the *Pietà* had made a deep impression on our family, we were stunned. How could someone deliberately do such a thing? This act was an affront to beauty itself. The human reaction to the destruction of beauty runs parallel to our reaction to evil. This kind of thing should not happen. One ought not to destroy such beauty.

It is not only when beautiful things are destroyed that we respond with aversion. We respond in that way to beauty's opposite, ugliness. When we encounter ugliness we think, "Things ought not to be this way." Ugliness, again like evil, distorts our humanity. It twists things that ought to be beautiful. It hinders our flourishing and thwarts our humanity. Toward the end of C. S. Lewis's *That Hideous Strength*, Professor Frost brings Mark Studdock into what is called the Objectifying Room. The purpose of this room is to eliminate every "subjective" attachment from Mark's soul:

> The room, at first sight, was an anticlimax. It appeared to be an empty committee room with a long table, eight or nine chairs, some picture, and (oddly enough) a large step-ladder in one corner. . . . A man of trained sensibility would have seen at once that the room was ill proportioned, not grotesquely so, but sufficiently to produce dislike. It was too high and too narrow. Mark felt the effect without analyzing the cause and the effect grew on him as the time passed.[6]

This room twists Mark's aesthetic expectations. The distribution of spots on the ceiling suggests but does not quite fit into a pattern. The pictures are realistic but contain surreal distortions such as hair inside the mouth of a woman. The plurality of distortions disquiets the mind: "He understood the whole business now. Frost was not trying to make him insane; at least not in the sense Mark had hitherto given to the word 'insanity.' Frost had meant what he said. To sit in the room was the first step towards what Frost called objectivity—the process whereby all specifically human reactions were killed in a man."[7] The tool to abolish Mark's humanity in this scenario is not outrageous ugliness. It is the small distortion, the slight twist, things bent away

---

[6]C. S. Lewis, *That Hideous Strength* (New York: Macmillan, 1946), 350-51.
[7]Ibid., 353.

from the beautiful. Through subtle but systematic disorder, the very reality of the good, the true, and the beautiful are all put under attack.

Things ought not to be this way. There is a way things should be, and this way includes beauty. Beauty, like goodness, is restorative. It affirms our humanity and contributes to our flourishing. Like goodness, beauty is good for us. We need beauty. There is something deeply moral about creating and protecting ordinary beauty. The Christian story holds that God is originator of all beautiful things and of those who participate in their creation and celebration. Beauty springs forth, is real, and we revel in it. There are things worth seeing because God is the Master Artist.

Nine

BEAUTY POINTS THE WAY HOME

When it comes to fiction, I read the same books over and over. My favorite authors are C. S. Lewis, Walker Percy, Jane Austen, and J. R. R. Tolkien. Every two or three years I work through all of the novels of Jane Austen and Walker Percy, much of Lewis's, and, of course, Tolkien's great work: *The Lord of the Rings*. Tolkien's trilogy is an epic journey that spans great distances through a number of realms, but it is most fundamentally about coming home. The last two chapters are the most important in the whole story. In the penultimate chapter, "The Scouring of the Shire," the four hobbits return to the Shire only to find their home under the thumb of the deposed wizard Saruman. The formerly hapless hobbits now emerge as confident leaders and quickly restore freedom and peace to their land. Over the next few years Frodo, who had sacrificed the most to overcome the evil of Sauron, finds that there is no rest in the Shire for him. He has saved it, but not for himself. In the final chapter, he sails away from Middle Earth with Gandalf, Bilbo, and the elves, never to return. After his ship disappears from sight, Sam, Merry, and Pippin, grief stricken, turn home:

> At last the three companions turned away, and never again looking back they rode slowly homewards; and they spoke no word to one another until they came back to the Shire, but each had great comfort in his friends on the long grey road.
>
> At last they rode over the downs and took the East Road, and then Merry and Pippin rode on to Buckland; and already they were singing again as they went. But Sam turned to Bywater, and so came back up the Hill, as day was ending once more. And he went on, and there was yellow light. And fire within; and the evening meal was ready, and he was expected. And Rose drew him in, and set him in his chair, and put little Elanor upon his lap.
>
> He drew a deep breath. "Well, I'm back," he said.[1]

This is a story about coming home. These last lines reveal that the story is Sam's story. The great battles and the rise and fall of kings make possible the return of an ordinary hobbit. Whenever I read this work, I choke up at these final lines. All of the adventures, dangers, and heroic deeds culminate in the simple return. Sam returns home to a meal, a fire in the fireplace, and family. Ordinary people fight against extraordinary obstacles because ordinary life matters. We travel great distances metaphorically or literally because coming home matters. In some ways we do not come to love home until we have taken the journey. In the lines of T. S. Eliot:

> We shall not cease from exploration
> And the end of all our exploring
> Will be to arrive where we started
> And know the place for the first time.[2]

---

[1]J. R. R. Tolkien, *The Return of the King* (Boston: Houghton Mifflin, 1955), 311.
[2]T. S. Eliot, *Four Quartets* (New York: Harcourt, Brace and World, 1943), 39.

C. S. Lewis wrote fittingly of Tolkien's work that "here are beauties which pierce like swords or burn like cold iron; here is a book that will break your heart."[3] Stories such as *The Lord of the Rings* awaken a longing within us. These longings themselves and not their satisfaction constitute the experience of beauty. No wonder we reread beautiful stories and beautiful poems. Beauty calls to us and stirs up desires for the journey and desires for the return home. This reality fits well into the Christian story: *In the Christian story, beauty points the way home.*

In the Christian story the way home lies in two directions. First, Christianity holds that our home is beyond this present world. We were made for a relationship with God that outlives our present life. But the Christian story also holds that *this* world is home. This world was made for us. We are, then, at home in two different places. Whether Christian or not, most people think Christianity points exclusively away from this world. Most assume that the Christian story teaches that we are not at home in this world, nor should we be. But the reality, goodness, and beauty of this world are consistent themes in Christian thinking. These features prompt us to recognize that this world comes from the hand of God. God created the world, in part, with us in mind.

Our experience of beauty resonates with the Christian story and whispers that there is a home for us here. How exactly does beauty reveal that this world is home? Roger Scruton explains: "The experience of natural beauty . . . contains a reassurance that this world is a right and fitting place to be—a home in which our human powers and prospects find confirmation."[4] Beauty contains a reassurance of our belonging. Our belonging in this world is captured in the story of our creation.

---

[3]C. S. Lewis, "Tolkien's *The Lord of the Rings*," in *On Stories and Other Essays on Literature*, ed. Walter Hooper (New York: Harcourt, 1966, 1982), 84.

[4]Roger Scruton, *Beauty: A Very Short Introduction* (Oxford: Oxford University Press, 2011), 55.

> Then the LORD God formed man from the dust of the ground, and breathed into his nostrils the breath of life; and the man became a living being. And the LORD God planted a garden in Eden, in the east; and there he put the man whom he had formed. Out of the ground the LORD God made to grow every tree that is pleasant to the sight and good for food, the tree of life also in the midst of the garden, and the tree of the knowledge of good and evil. . . . The LORD God took the man and put him in the garden of Eden to till it and keep it. (Gen 2:7-9, 15)

As we have seen, the Christian story begins with God creating a good world and creating human beings to bear the divine image. God made a garden and placed human beings into it. God did not put us into the "formless void" (Gen 1:2). God prepared a world fitting for human beings and fitting for our purposes. God's purposes for us involve using the capacities that mirror the divine nature in order to cultivate the good world into which God has placed us. We have been placed in a garden, and we are to till it and keep it. Our purpose of bringing and experiencing flourishing is to be pursued in this world.

This feature of God's creative activity explains why we find ourselves at home in this world. Our work, our relationships, our creative endeavors, and our moral aspirations have all been made with this world in mind. It is a good and beautiful arena to become the people we are meant to become. God's plan, as we have said, includes our continuing the creation task. We are to bring good, true, useful, and beautiful things out of this good world. This world is a fitting place for us.

The Christian story indicates that we are at home in this world, but at the same time we are restless for another world. Human rebellion against God has distorted the goodness of all creation. Our own ability to live well is corrupted. Our ability to bring good out of the world is damaged. Augustine observed that, morally, we are mired both in ignorance and in difficulty. People find it difficult to embody the virtues they should "either because they do not see how they ought to be, or because they lack the power to be what they see they ought to be."[5] That it is hard to practice the virtues we ought to is clear. We have discussed how we habituate ourselves into patterns of choosing and acting. These patterns reveal that we have become bent in on ourselves.

Our disordered state not only has affected our moral and spiritual features, but it has distorted our creative capacities. Our work, relationships, and artistic endeavors are each infected with this self-focus. We are not able to bring unalloyed good things out of the world. As Andy Crouch has observed, while cultural goods always make something possible that was impossible, "culture can make some things impossible that were previously possible."[6] Our contribution to the world is mixed.

The world itself has also been distorted. It is not the way it ought to be. After Adam rejected God, God spoke to him:

> Cursed is the ground because of you;
>   in toil you shall eat of it all the days of your life;
> thorns and thistles it shall bring forth for you;
>   and you shall eat the plants of the field.
> By the sweat of your face
>   you shall eat bread
> until you return to the ground,
>   for out of it you were taken;
> you are dust,
>   and to dust you shall return. (Gen 3:17-19)

[5]Augustine, *On Free Choice of the Will*, trans. Thomas Williams (Indianapolis: Hackett, 1983), 3.18.

[6]Andy Crouch, *Culture Making: Recovering Our Creative Calling* (Downers Grove, IL: InterVarsity Press, 2008), 28.

We are now estranged from our home. Note that God does not revoke the call to cultivate the world. The call remains, but this task is now riddled with difficulties. The world is not as openly responsive to human cultivation as it once was. Tilling our garden requires toil and brings sweat. In addition, we are embroiled in a pervasive conflict between good and evil. We are reminded of the complexity of this conflict by Russian novelist Aleksandr Solzhenitsyn: "If only it were so simple! If only there were evil people somewhere insidiously committing evil deeds, and it were necessary only to separate them from the rest of us and destroy them. But the line dividing good and evil cuts through the heart of every human being. And who is willing to destroy a piece of his own heart?"[7] Each of us is divided within. We are naturally exploitive rather than cooperative. We exert our own power at the expense of others. We are fragmented beings.

These challenges stir a longing for restoration and healing. We long for peace, goodness, and justice. We long for the world to be made right. We are saddened by its corruption, and we grieve the evil that twists and destroys so many good things. In short, we long for the next life, in which all of the corruption will be healed. We are still in some sense at home in this world, but we are restless for another. There is a deep connection between this world and the next in the Christian story. The next world includes the healing of all the ills of this one. Rather than holding forth a divided picture, the Christian story unites this world with the next.

Beauty stirs this restlessness for another world. No one, perhaps, took this aspect of beauty further than Plato. Plato argued that beauty is the ultimate end at which love aims. Love, he explained, is a passion to possess forever the good and the beautiful. In his dialogue *The Symposium* the prophetess Diotima reveals to Socrates the real purpose

[7]Aleksandr I. Solzhenitsyn, *The Gulag Archipelago: An Experiment in Literary Investigation*, trans. Thomas P. Whitney (New York: Harper and Row, 1973), 1:168.

of love: "It is giving birth in beauty, whether in body or in soul."[8] To give birth in beauty is to be moved to bring forth beautiful things in response to the presence of beauty. Plato describes how beauty launches us on a journey or an ascent. We are moved to recognize that individual people or things may *share in* beauty, but they are not beauty itself. Love moves us, then, to turn from the variety of beautiful things we discern with our senses, in order to grasp beauty itself. Beauty, for Plato, is a Form. It is that reality that makes all particular beautiful things beautiful. Beauty itself is more real than any particular beautiful thing. Like other Forms, such as holiness, justice, and goodness, beauty is outside space and time. Growing in wisdom involves moving from being captured by particular beautiful things to contemplating the Form of beauty itself. Plato thought that the encounter with beauty prompted creative action, longing, and contemplation. Of these three, the greatest is contemplation. For Plato, contemplation of the Form of beauty, and all of the Forms, is the end or goal of human life:

> "But how would it be, in our view," Diotima said, "if someone got to see the Beautiful itself, absolute, pure, unmixed, not polluted by human flesh or colors or any other great nonsense of mortality, but if he could see the divine Beauty itself in its one form? Do you think it would be a poor life for a human being to look there and to behold it by that which he ought, and to be with it?"[9]

Not many thinkers agree with all of Plato's thoughts about love and beauty. For Plato, this world is *not* a fitting home for us. It is a hindrance to our purpose. The wise person aims to escape this world in order to encounter the real world—the world beyond the physical, beyond space and time. The real world is not the realm of particular things that happen to be beautiful. It is the realm of beauty itself. Thus

---

[8]Plato, *Symposium*, trans. Alexander Nehamas and Paul Woodruff (Indianapolis: Hackett, 1989), 206b.
[9]Ibid., 211e-212a.

we may begin with loving the beauty of some particular person, but we must learn to love the abstract beauty if we are to encounter true beauty.

We will most likely reject the notion that we ought to leave *particular* good and beautiful things behind as we dance with beauty itself. Love, we think, is always particular. Plato does, however, describe a reality that requires an account. We are captured by beauty in ways that go deeper than the fact that it satisfies us. It triggers a *dissatisfaction*. It brings out a longing that draws us onward. It does lift our eyes and it moves us to creative action, longing, and contemplation. We can see how Plato's thought contributed to the idea that beauty is a transcendental. He thought that beauty lifts our gaze up beyond the normal objects of our vision to the things that are most real.

For Plato, there is really only one world. The present world of space and time is barely real at all. There is no real knowledge of things in space and time. At best we can have opinions.[10] In atheistic stories there is also only one world. The real world in these views, contrary to Plato, *is* the world of space and time. Beyond this world, there is no other. The longings that beauty triggers for another world are longings without proper objects. Such longings remind us that we are not quite at home here.

In Jean-Paul Sartre's novel *Nausea*, the character Roquentin is mired in the struggle to manage his own meaninglessness in an absurd universe. "So this is Nausea: this blinding evidence? I have scratched my head over it! I've written about it. Now I know: I exist—the world exists—and I know that the world exists. That's all. It makes no difference to me."[11] It does not matter whether he lives or dies. His work as a historian no longer has any bearing on his life. He is isolated and barely manages to hold conversations with those around him. He records that "every existing thing is born without

[10]See Plato, *Republic* 476c-477b.

[11]Jean-Paul Sartre, *Nausea*, trans. Lloyd Alexander (New York: New Directions Paperback, 1959), 122.

reason, prolongs itself out of weakness and dies by chance."[12] In a long conversation, his former lover, Anny, describes her search for the perfect moment. She was looking to the perfect moment in order to make her life feel meaningful:

> "That's it," she says. "First you had to be plunged into something exceptional and feel as though you were putting it in order. If all those conditions had been realized, the moment would have been perfect."
>
> "In fact, it was a sort of work of art."
>
> "You've already said that," she says with irritation. "No: it was . . . a duty. You *had* to transform privileged situations into perfect moments. It was a moral question. Yes, you can laugh if you like: it was moral."[13]

Later in the conversation, she admits that the search for the perfect moment is futile: "That's it. There are no adventures—there are no perfect moments."[14] Roquentin tries to salvage this search through art, through her acting:

> "But weren't you ever carried away by your part?"
>
> "A little, sometimes: never very strongly. The essential thing, for all of us, was the black pit just in font of us, in the bottom of it there were people you didn't see; obviously you were presenting them with a perfect moment. But, you know, they didn't live in it: it unfolded in front of them. And we, the actors, do you think we lived inside it? In the end, it wasn't anywhere, not on either side of the footlights, it didn't exist; and yet everybody thought about it. So you see, little man," she says in a dragging, almost vulgar tone of voice, "I walked out on the whole business."[15]

---

[12]Ibid., 133.
[13]Ibid., 148.
[14]Ibid., 150.
[15]Ibid., 152.

The performance promised the perfect moment for the audience, but it failed this promise. They could observe a moment, but they could not live inside it. The striving for a perfect moment turned out to be vain. Beauty may trigger longings for something beyond this world or this life. In an atheistic world, that longing is empty. As we saw in chapter three, the things we care most about are least at home in the atheistic picture of reality. Our dreams, our hopes, and our picture of ourselves do not fit. They may mock us, but they do not lead us anywhere. They may reveal that we are, in Walker Percy's words, "lost in the cosmos."[16] They do not point the way home. They do not point at all.

In the Christian story, our longings are clues. They are not always reliable, but they tend to indicate that something more is afoot. They are not inexplicable emotions or superfluous features of a meaningless universe. There *are* two worlds. Both are real. Our longings point in both directions. We are at home in two places. C. S. Lewis expresses well how our longings have real objects that satisfy them:

> Creatures are not born with desires unless satisfaction for these desires exists. A baby feels hunger: well, there is such a thing as food. A duckling wants to swim: well, there is such a thing as water. Men feel sexual desire: well, there is such a thing as sex. If I find in myself a desire which no experience in this world can satisfy, the most probable explanation is that I was made for another world. If none of my earthly pleasures satisfy it, that does not prove that the universe is a fraud. Probably earthly pleasures were never meant to satisfy it, but only to arouse it, to suggest the real thing.[17]

---

[16]Walker Percy, *Lost in the Cosmos: The Last Self-Help Book* (New York: Farrar, Straus and Giroux, 1983).

[17]C. S. Lewis, *Mere Christianity* (New York: Scribner, 1952), 106.

There are two temptations that we can fall into when we think about the place of beauty in the scheme of things. The first is the temptation to take a minimal stance. Beauty, we might say, is simply a cultural artifact, and judgments concerning beauty reflect subjective assessments and nothing more. Beauty, after all, is in the eye of the beholder. As such, any judgment of beauty is solely a matter of the preference or experience of the one who judges. So beauty is a matter of preference, and our preferences are shaped by all of the contours of our personal histories and of our cultural moment.

The other temptation is to worship beauty. We can ascribe to it nearly divine status and power. Beauty encounters us and lifts us to a different plane of being. We enter a realm that bursts with meaning and purpose. Beauty opens the door to a deeper truth about ourselves and our place in the world. In this way beauty safeguards and grounds the meaning of our lives. Our humanness in an otherwise impersonal cosmos is affirmed.

These two temptations can be active within us at the same time. We may strive to extract a significant sense of meaning from our experiences of beauty, while at the same time we may affirm an allegiance to certain theories or to a worldview that has no place for beauty apart from the subjective. These two temptations pull in opposite directions. They do not sit well together. Hence we can be conflicted about beauty.

It is, perhaps, too simplistic to call the first temptation a product of the Enlightenment and the second a product of Romanticism, but these intellectual movements do support the underlying pulls that we feel in these contrary directions. If the Enlightenment can be summarized with the quip *Sapere aude* or "Dare to be wise,"[18] Romanticism might be characterized by "Dare to imagine" or "Dare to feel." The first emphasizes the pursuit of knowledge based on reason rather than on

[18]Immanuel Kant, "An Answer to the Question: What Is Enlightenment?," trans. H. B. Nisbet, repr. in *From Modernism to Postmodernism: An Anthology*, ed. Lawrence Cahoone (Oxford: Blackwell, 1996), 51.

tradition or authority. The second emphasizes the cultivation of aesthetic experience. Romanticism holds a deep commitment to freedom both in art and in life, from the confines of the structures of inherited or classical forms. Knowledge is not rejected in Romanticism. Rather, our emotive and aesthetic experiences are seen to be means to knowledge about the most important aspects of our humanity.

The Romantic notion that beauty is divine, I believe, is closer to the truth about reality. Beauty is something that *is* transcendental. Beauty points beyond the realm of our experiences to something more permanent. The idea that beauty has this pointing role resonates with Christian thinking. Beauty is not God, but God—the source of all beauty—has instilled a desire for beauty within us. Beauty is a signpost. In the Christian story, beauty points the way home.

Part IV

FREEDOM

Ten

PERSONAL FREEDOM

"Freedom, that's just some people talking. Your prison is walking through this world all alone."[1] The Eagles's song "Desperado" well expresses the ambiguities of freedom. In this classic story of a Western outlaw, freedom from capture comes at a high cost. The desperado is always on the run. He walks through the world alone. One kind of freedom is another kind of prison.

What is freedom? We apply the term in a variety of ways. In political contexts we think a society is free if it allows its citizens significant participation in the political process. Often we identify political freedom with a set of secure rights that aim to protect citizens. The foundational rights in democratic societies involve freedom of speech, freedom from arbitrary exercise of authority, freedom of religious conscience, and other similar guarantees. These rights are so deeply ingrained in our concept of political freedom that often we categorize a nation as free only if these kinds of rights are safeguarded.

Freedom is also a philosophical concept. We ask whether human beings are free as opposed to being determined. This question is about whether a person's actions are up to him in a significant sense

[1]Eagles, "Desperado," by Glenn Frey and Don Henley, on *Desperado*, Alfred Music Publishing, 1973.

or whether they are entirely a result of previous causal factors. Many philosophers think that we need some level of significant freedom in order to be morally responsible. There are many disagreements about what significant freedom amounts to or even whether we have such freedom.

The kind of freedom that is captured by songs such as "Desperado" can be called *personal freedom*. Personal freedom is completely independent of philosophical freedom. No matter what theory you hold about determinism and philosophical freedom, you will care about personal freedom. Political freedom is more closely related to personal freedom, but the two are not the same. Even if we have our basic political freedoms protected, we may still feel like we walk in bondage. We all *long* to be free, but what is it exactly that we long for?

Aristotle writes that everyone agrees that the highest good is happiness and that they "understand being happy as equivalent to living well and acting well."[2] He observes that people generally have some idea about what a good life looks like. The good life is marked by personal freedom. Freedom involves the ability to pursue and to accomplish the things that are important to us.

Aristotle is right that we long for a certain kind of life, one that is rich and rewarding. He is also correct that we share some ideas about what goes into the best life. If I am honest, I must admit that there are moments in which I think a rich life amounts to a comfortable life. I want to sit on our back patio with a cup of coffee or a glass of red wine (depending on the time of day) and chat with Jeanie or read a book. While there is nothing wrong with these activities, I recognize that these desires are comfort desires. They are vacation longings. My deeper longings are not for perpetual leisure. I want to invest in work that I take to be important. I want to invest in the people I love. I want to be a person who embodies the virtues that I ought to embody.

---

[2]Aristotle, *Nicomachean Ethics*, trans. Roger Crisp (Cambridge: Cambridge University Press, 2000), book 1, chap. 4, 1095a, 18.

Previously we discussed the notion of core identity. My core identity involves my deepest desires about who I am and who I long to be. When I give it careful thought, I realize that my deeper longings are not simply vacation longings. I want something more. I want to be a certain kind of person. I want a life that is centered on what is real, what is beautiful, and what is good. I want a life filled with relationships with other people that are characterized by trust, love, security, and fun. My deeper longings are for something much more than comfort and pleasure. In previous sections, I suggested that we long for goodness and beauty and that our deepest concerns always involve persons. Goodness, beauty, and rich relationships are features of a full and rewarding life. Love, goodness, and beauty constitute the way things ought to be. Thus they contribute to a life that is a good human life. A life without love, goodness, and beauty is impoverished.

What it means to be free or to flourish as a human being depends a good deal on the nature of human beings. Aristotle also recognized this truth. He argued that there is a function to human nature. There are objective ways that the human person runs well. These ways are connected to what it is to be a human being. Aristotle uses the example of a knife. Just as there are qualities that make a knife excellent, there are qualities that make a person's life excellent.[3] The Greek word for "excellence" can also mean "virtue." The qualities that make a human life excellent are the virtues. These virtues are not limited to moral virtues. For Aristotle, to be a person of wisdom, prudence, generosity, and courage, among other things, is to be a person who flourishes. Of course, there are many different views about human nature. We have canvassed some of these in this book. The list of things you count as virtues will depend on the view you have about what it means to be a person. Your set of virtues will include the qualities that help any of us achieve the best life possible given the sort of beings we are.

---

[3]Ibid., book 1, chap. 7, 1097b, 23-33.

Personal freedom, then, is connected to virtue. We experience greater freedom as we become the people we ought to be. If this is the case, then the best life is much less dependent on what is happening around us than we often think. Our freedom depends more on the kind of people we are. As I become a more patient person, for example, I am less at the mercy of the circumstances around me. Perhaps I can even drive on the Southern California freeways without getting angry. Personal freedom is, in a strong sense, *internal* freedom. It is the freedom to be or to become a person of excellence, whatever our circumstances.

Our situation in life is not completely irrelevant to our freedom, however. External oppression can crush a person. Extreme poverty, for example, can make it nearly impossible to pursue other goods in life. Suffering disrupts our stability. But understanding personal freedom in terms of becoming the people we ought to be helps us see that there is more to what we want than vacation desires. We want to be free to live out the qualities of excellent human beings.

To say that personal freedom is internal, however, is not to say that it is solitary. A person's excellence finds its expression in the relationships that are most important to her. As we saw above, relationships are vital to our deepest desires about the best life. My ability to enter and sustain rich relationships is largely a matter of my practice of relational and moral virtues. As I practice these excellences, I help others on the path to living well.

What we want is personal freedom. We long for the sense that we are becoming who we want to be. We want to live lives of excellence. We long to embody those qualities that make our lives rich and our relationships fulfilling. We want to walk well, and we do not want to walk through the world alone.

Eleven

FREEDOM AND TRUTH

I once saw a bumper sticker that read "Language Is Not Transparent." I paused. . . . Perhaps language is not *perfectly* transparent, but it is transparent enough. In fact, if it were not sufficiently transparent, I would not have been able to understand the message. I did not have to work very hard to find the meaning of the statement. I did not wonder whether it was a claim about the driver's favorite political candidate or about the Red Sox. I was confident that I got the message. I knew that it was a particular claim and that it was a claim about language. I grasped all of this at a glance, going fifty-five—okay, maybe sixty-five—miles per hour on the Wilbur Cross Parkway in Connecticut. Language is transparent enough.

When someone makes a claim such as "language is not transparent," what is she trying to say? The human capacity to use language is as common as anything in our experience. Every culture is a language culture. We use symbols (sounds and shapes) for a variety of purposes, including stating what we take to be facts, issuing commands, asking questions, and expressing emotions. So I can represent a small chunk of the world with a statement such as "My cup is on the table." I can represent that piece of the world truly or falsely.

Human communication about simple facts is more complicated than sending a signal, such as the kind of warning that crows or dogs can send to one another. It can do more than these signals. There is an abstraction that is involved. My sentence *represents* a fact involving some object (the cup) and some true things about that object (it is on the table). The nouns refer to objects, and the predicates describe their relations to one another.

Human beings do not use language only to describe small chunks of the world. We use language to make requests, to express our preferences, and to share grief. We construct complicated theories about the way the world is. We entertain possibilities about the way the world might in fact be or could have been. We construct fictional worlds and populate them with hobbits and wizards. We describe reality, we make up stories, we sing songs, we write poetry. We express love and concern to others, we warn each other, and we pass down our cherished beliefs and practices to our children and grandchildren. Language is fundamentally interpersonal. I can represent the world *to you.* All of these activities involve the use of language. We navigate and celebrate the world together as we speak together.

The claim that language is not transparent is not likely to be directed against the poetic or imaginative uses of language. I suspect that it is directed against the use of language to make claims about what is real. I cannot pretend that I know what the person had in mind when the bumper sticker was chosen. I really don't know. But given the nature of bumper-sticker slogans and some widely held cultural notions, I would guess that the sticker reflects a worry about people who make truth claims. The sticker is sort of a reminder, "You might think you are making a straightforward claim about the world, but remember, *language is not transparent!*"

The bumper sticker expresses a claim about the meaning-carrying capacity of language. It expresses a worry over the ability of language to articulate truth. Such worries circulate regularly in our culture—

especially in some branches of academic culture. Postmodernism as a cultural or philosophical set of commitments involves concerns about the way we make truth claims. One of the most common concerns includes the idea that it is now simply impossible to talk about truth in traditional ways. We have learned, presumably, that the notion of having our claims represent the world accurately is naive. All of our truth claims are infected with our cultural assumptions so that we cannot hope to match the world as it is in itself. Some thinkers add to this view the further claim that there is no world in itself. Reality itself, they think, is largely socially constructed. Therefore, to make a truth claim is stifling or oppressive to those who disagree with you. If someone thinks his claim is *true* in a real or objective sense, he must also think competing claims are *false*. It appears wrong or almost immoral to think that another person's belief is false. It seems rude or arrogant. Thinking that one knows the truth about some important issue is what causes much of the bitter disagreement we see in the world. Some think that if we can avoid making and holding such truth claims, we can work toward developing cooperation rather than causing conflict.

A second concern is a corollary to the first. It is the idea that people who make truth claims have self-serving reasons for making them. If truth claims cannot match reality, there must be other reasons at work. These reasons are not straightforward. Rather than evaluating a person's claim, we aim to uncover their actual motives. Our posture, then, is one of suspicion. Rather than listening to one another, we aim to reveal one another. We see this practice in journalism and the many heated discussions that erupt on social media.

Not all of academic culture has been taken with these worries over truth. Postmodernism completely bypassed large chunks of the academic world. In analytic philosophy, for example, traditional notions of truth are widely, though not universally, considered to be right. Those working in the hard sciences and in subjects such as mathematics for the most part also continue to think about truth in more or less traditional ways. Sometimes scholars in these latter fields limit the scope of objective truth to questions that are answered through methods that are sufficiently similar to those used in science or mathematics. This limitation is often described in terms of a distinction between facts and values. Claims of fact can be true or false, while claims of value cannot.

These philosophical and cultural movements leave us with prevalent worries about truth. The first, coming out of the postmodern influence, is the concern that even believing that some position is true is an arrogant or oppressive move. Second, influenced by those outside the reach of postmodernism, there is concern that while truth is important in some realms of learning, people often make and defend truth claims in areas where truth does not actually apply. Often it is in the arena of moral discussions that both of these trends are seen. Moral disagreements easily get mired in accusations of arrogance. In addition, many people think that there is not a truth of the matter in a moral dispute.

All the same, it is a persistent feature of the human experience that we strive to come to know and to say what is true. Despite these theoretical objections to traditional approaches to truth, it is something we deeply care about. Not only is coming to know what is true important to us, but it is connected deeply with personal freedom. What we want in life is tied up with what is true about life.

Nietzsche helped to fuel both suspicion and animosity surrounding the whole truth project.[1] We already encountered Nietzsche's view that the practice of making moral judgments hinders human flourishing. I introduced his notion of the ascetic ideal, the idea that we have to give up our passions and drives for something more important, such as goodness. The ascetic ideal, for Nietzsche, is not limited to the

---

[1]Some of my discussion here is derived from my chapter "Nietzsche," in *Christian Theology and the Modern Philosophers*, ed. Benjamin H. Arbour and Gregory E. Ganssle (Grand Rapids: Zondervan, forthcoming).

moral or religious areas of life. Nietzsche raises the question of where opposition to the ascetic ideal is to be found. He launches his criticism of the ascetic ideal in such a way that the reader assumes it to be a challenge to traditional morality and of Christianity. Toward the end of *On the Genealogy of Morality*, he turns on those who may be tempted to see his point as an affirmation of scientific rationalism against religion.[2] Nietzsche claims that science itself is "not opposite the ascetic ideal but rather the latter's own most *recent and noble manifestation*."[3] He goes on to say, "Our faith in science is still based on a *metaphysical faith*."[4] Why is science no antidote to the ascetic ideal? Because science, just as much as religion and morality, is grounded in the will to truth.[5]

The ascetic ideal is not merely a religious ideal. It is the dominant story of Western intellectual history. From Plato to the present, not just goodness and a right relationship with God but knowledge itself has been thought to be an ideal to which we must aspire. We must sacrifice to achieve this ideal. This notion is a metaphysical faith because it is the faith that truth is of ultimate value, that truth is divine. If truth is divine, then we must sacrifice anything that stands in the way of attaining truth.

It is important to see that Nietzsche's challenge to the will to truth is not based only on the idea that truth is not attainable. He is challenging the will to truth because this will is *life denying*. The will to truth is life denying because the very things that make up life must be left behind in the quest for the objective (as opposed to a subjective) truth. The scientific pursuit of knowledge objectifies everything, including the scientist herself. When the scientist studies human beings, they become objects like fruit flies under a microscope. The person

---

[2]Friedrich Nietzsche, *On the Genealogy of Morality*, ed. Keith Ansell-Pearson, trans. Carol Diethe, Cambridge Texts in the History of Political Thought (Cambridge: Cambridge University Press, 1994), 3.23.

[3]Ibid., 3.23. Italics original.

[4]Ibid., 3.24. Italics original.

[5]Ibid., 3.25, 27.

herself is removed from the investigation. She is just an organism. It is, however, precisely on the level of an individual and her drives or needs that life is found. To leave behind the individual's passions and concerns is to leave behind all that affirms life.

Underneath it all, Nietzsche probably thinks that there are some objective truths. His criticism of science as being infected with the ascetic ideal should be seen as a criticism of how science proceeded in his day. Nietzsche's criticisms apply to the science of our day as well. Science, for Nietzsche, is not naturalistic enough. It simply *assumes* that the world operates with law-like regularities and that we can discover them. The best practices of science should leave us with the realization that all claims turn out to be mere interpretations. For example, that the world operates with law-like regularities is not something that we discovered. It is a claim that we invented and imposed on the world. It is our interpretation. All interpretations are put forward to achieve the *will to power*. If I fail to embrace that all claims aim at the will to power, I will fail to embrace life itself. I turn my back on the prime opportunity to express my own will to power. I am allowing the alleged objectivity of reality to stand over me. I am placing myself as subservient to something outside me.

If Nietzsche fueled suspicion and animosity about truth, the roots of the fact-value dichotomy can be traced to David Hume. Hume claimed that *reason* produces only two kinds of judgments. He called these "relations of ideas" and "matters of fact."[6] Relations of ideas consist of things that we know without consulting experience. Claims such as "1+1=2" or "No bachelor is married" fit into this category. These judgments analyze what is already contained in the subject. Once we understand what *bachelor* is, we can see that no bachelor is married. We do not have to inspect a sample of bachelors to see

---

[6]David Hume, *An Enquiry Concerning Human Understanding*, ed. L. A. Selby-Bigge (Oxford: Oxford University Press, 1902), originally published in 1748. See section 4, part 1, p. 24.

whether they are in fact unmarried. Matters of fact, on the other hand, are those claims that can be supported only by consulting experience. We must look and see whether the claim is true. If I claim that my coffee has grown cold, I am making a claim that purports to be a matter of fact. It might be true, and it might be false. We have to look and see. The only kind of evidence that supports a claim that is a matter of fact is the evidence of our experience. We cannot analyze the nature of coffee and determine that my coffee has grown cold.

When we are trying to answer a question, Hume thinks we must first determine what sort of answer we are looking for. Is it a matter of fact, or is it a relation of ideas? If it purports to be a matter of fact, we ask, "What experience would count as evidence for this claim?" If the claim is about facts in the world, we must be able to identify some experience of the five senses that could count as evidence. If the claim is about our inner state, such as whether or not we are angry or are thinking about pizza, we need to identify an *inner* experience. If we cannot discern any experience that would count as evidence, the claim turns out not to be a claim of reason. Therefore, it is not the sort of thing that can be true or false.

Hume invites his reader to observe a crime such as a murder. What we will observe, he thinks, is the series of events that results in the death of the victim. We never experience the moral wrongness of the act of murder. Thus claims about moral wrongness are not matters of fact. Moral values do not reflect reality in the way that empirical claims do. Hume assumed that facts in the world are limited to the sorts of things that can be justified by the methods of science or other empirical methods, while values and metaphysical claims are not able to be true or false. They wind up being reduced to cultural or individual preferences. Those who hold this kind of view do not challenge the traditional notion of truth. They restrict the application of truth to claims that are subject to confirmation either by analysis or by experience.

There is no question that these ideas have trickled down and spread throughout our culture. Despite how common these notions have become, it is worth challenging them. We can begin by pointing out that each of these positions is made up of a number of truth claims. Nietzsche's claims, then, ought to be interpreted as being infected with his own cultural assumptions. If so, his assertions should not necessarily be persuasive to us. Furthermore, he appears to think that his view is correct and the traditional view is false. On his own account his assertions are simply exercises in exerting his own will to power. Why, then, should we accept his claims? To return to the bumper sticker, if language is not transparent, then the language used to challenge a traditional view of truth also is not transparent.

The distinction Hume makes between what really counts as a matter of fact and what only purports to be a matter of fact but fails to be so is a distinction that his own view cannot justify. First, it is not a matter of definition or analysis that facts must be able to be justified by experience. Nor can this claim be justified by some particular experience. According to Hume's own scheme, then, his position is not rationally grounded. Therefore he has provided no *reason* to think that there cannot be facts about goodness and evil or about what sorts of people we ought to be. Both Nietzsche and Hume challenge our thinking about truth. The limitations they put on our approaches to truth and to reason, however, are undermined by their own criteria.

The fact of the matter is that we cannot help but make truth claims. Furthermore, we do not, and perhaps we cannot, limit our truth claims to empirical issues. Nor do we limit our claims to things of only immediate practical concern. Hume recognized that we have the ingrained practice of making the sort of judgments that lie outside the scope of reason. This practice explains why we continue to think there are truths in the realm of metaphysics and ethics, even if there are none. He attributes this practice to *habit*. Our concern for these kinds of truths, however, appears to be more than simply a habit that is unrelated to reason. We are deeply truth oriented. If we are right to reject Hume's restrictions about the kinds of claims that can be true, we can continue to navigate the world in light of what it is truly good to be and to do. We think there *are* truths about the kind of people we should be, and we navigate the world accordingly.

That we can challenge Nietzsche and Hume about truth is crucial. It does not, however, resolve these difficulties for most people. The fact remains that we are ambivalent about truth. On the one hand, we order our lives around what we take to be true. On the other, we are suspicious of truth claims. Our suspicion is deep and is not put to rest by answering Nietzsche and Hume. So why are we suspicious about truth? To be honest, I think that it is not really *truth* about which we are suspicious. We are suspicious about *people* who claim to know truth or to tell us what is true. As I admitted, I am resistant to evaluation. We want to *be* good or to *know* what is true, but we do not want to be corrected or taught by someone else. When someone thinks they have found the truth, especially about morality or God or how best to live, it makes us uneasy. We might think there are truths about these things, but, most likely, we do not think this other person has found them. Even if we grant that someone has found this kind of truth, we think she ought to keep it to herself. We worry that someone who thinks she already knows these things is poised to compel us to follow her or to believe what she believes. People who already have the truth want us to think the way they think. We want to be free to think the way we want to think. It is in this way that truth itself can be associated in our minds with oppression.

Despite these worries, we do want to find whatever truth we can about the world and our place in it. No one really wants to close his eyes to facts that might shape how he lives. I don't think any reflective person would deny this simple claim. So we are conflicted about the desirability of truth. As one student I knew said, "It is popular to search for truth, but it is not popular to find it." Searching sounds more open-minded than finding.

We have mentioned that all human beings share the same project. That project is the distinctly human activity of navigating the world in terms of reality. We all aim to be and to do the things that we think really are good to be and to do. Our ambivalence about truth leads to another observation about Christian theism: *In the Christian story, truth is good for us.* We saw previously that, in the Christian story, *goodness* is good for us. Now we see that truth and the pursuit of truth also contribute to our flourishing.

Perhaps the most famous statement of Jesus about truth is found in John's writings, where Jesus says, "The truth will make you free" (Jn 8:32). Here he explicitly links freedom with truth. Furthermore, the context of the discussion shows that the truth in question is not limited to empirical truth. It is religious and moral truth as well:

> "If you continue in my word, you are truly my disciples; and you will know the truth, and the truth will make you free." They answered him, "We are descendants of Abraham and have never been slaves to anyone. What do you mean by saying, 'You shall be made free'?"
>
> Jesus answered them, "Very truly, I tell you, everyone who commits sin is a slave to sin." (Jn 8:31-34)

To grasp what Jesus is saying here, we must think again about what he meant by the term *sin*. As we have seen, the Christian story includes the idea that human beings are created purposefully by God. We are made for relationship. We are made for a mutual relationship with each other and for a dependence relationship with the Creator. We choose either to live in this dependence relationship with God or to walk away. Sin is the walking away. Throughout the Scriptures, sin is fundamentally rejecting our dependence on God. Actions that might be called sins are manifestations of this fundamental rejection.

Now why might Jesus insist that rejecting our dependence on God brings slavery? Since we were created for the purpose of relationship with God, we fulfill our purpose in that relationship. We were made for love relationships with one another that are characterized by mutual service. As a result, we experience our purpose and our freedom in those relationships. Our rejection of God's purposes ruptures our relationships not only with God but with one another, with ourselves, and with the rest of created reality. Anything that disrupts our dependence on God disrupts our purpose and our flourishing. We walk away, and we step out of the source of freedom. This is how sin produces slavery. The person who steps out of the source of flourishing is not fully free to flourish.

If it is sin that oppresses, what is it that liberates? Jesus' answer is directly contrary to Nietzsche's. What liberates is truth. "The truth will make you free." How does the truth liberate? I think that there are several levels to what Jesus means about the truth liberating. I want to bring up two. On one level, the truth liberates for the simple reason that an accurate diagnosis of what oppresses is necessary to any successful view of human freedom. The people to whom Jesus first declared that everyone who sins is a slave to sin had completely misdiagnosed their condition. They thought of freedom and slavery only in political terms. They did not recognize that their own rejection of God caused them to be oppressed. They needed to gain some understanding about their condition before they could have any hope of being liberated. Whether or not Jesus' diagnosis about sin is correct, the principle stands. An accurate diagnosis of what is wrong is necessary in order to understand what will make it right. It is in this way that truth liberates.

On a broader level, truth liberates because the best life requires a life oriented toward reality. Here the view of Jesus contrasts with that of Hume. The task of navigating life with a view toward flourishing raises the question of what reality is. What sort of person I should be depends on what sort of thing a human being is in reality. It depends also on what moral reality is like, if there is any. It depends on whether there are facts about human purpose. Answers to these questions about our condition underlie any plausible idea about what sort of persons we should be. Such answers go beyond the domain of the empirical world.

The quest for the best human life is firmly embedded in the assumption that there are truths in the realm of values, including moral values. We engage every aspect of the world with our reason. In fact, the truths about what is good and worthy and the best to pursue are the truths that are most important to our freedom. Truth liberates in that truth about these issues will give us a solid foundation for making our way through life. We can navigate competing values and priorities and have some success at flourishing if we are doing so with moral, theological, psychological, and metaphysical reality in mind.

One way to diagnose a thinker's views on what promotes human flourishing is to ask, what promotes life, and what denies life? What oppresses? What liberates? Nietzsche taught that what promotes life is the rejection of any external standard, whether of morality or of truth. The ascetic ideal is the enemy of freedom. Nietzsche thought that the will to truth was part of what oppresses. Only in breaking free of these confines can an individual become what he ought to become. We find that Nietzsche's view resonates with the way we are resistant to truth claims that come from the outside.

In contrast to Nietzsche, Jesus articulates a vision in which *truth* liberates. Nietzsche thought that exerting the will to power is what liberates. Jesus thought that to exert our own power at the expense of another reveals that we are enslaved. It is a characteristic of disordered loves. To pursue such action is to miss life altogether. In contrast to Hume, Jesus taught that the truth that liberates goes beyond the empirical realm. It includes moral truth and religious truth. It is truth about what it means to be human. Jesus' vision, we can see, is more plausible than these alternative views. That truth is good for us makes sense of our shared project of navigating the world with a view to achieving the best human life. Truth does not oppress. It sets us free. Once again, we see that the Christian story makes sense of the things we care about most deeply.

Twelve

FREEDOM AND HOPE

I remember seeing a comic in a humor magazine in which four teenagers were surrounded by musical instruments. One said, "I think our recording contract should be with Capital Records." Another commented, "When we make our first film we should use the same director the Beatles used in *Help!*" (Okay, this was a *long* time ago!) A third talked about being interviewed in *Time* magazine. In the final panel, one looked at the instruments and commented, "Now, we just need to learn to play these things!" It is easy to be captured by big plans, but it takes something more to accomplish them.

Aristotle reminds us that it is *living* well rather than *thinking about* living well that matters: "Our present inquiry does not aim, as our others do, at study; for the purpose of our examination is not to know what virtue is, but to become good, since otherwise the inquiry would be of no benefit to us."[1] We navigate the world with the aim of becoming people of excellence. That is, we aim at being and doing good, not just at thinking about what is good. Becoming good is not easy. Doing anything well that is worth doing is not easy. We can talk about it, and we can dream about it, but consistent practice is challenging.

---

[1]Aristotle, *Nicomachean Ethics*, in *The Basic Works of Aristotle*, ed. Richard McKeon (New York: Random House, 1941), book 2, chap. 2., 1103b, 28-30.

Thus freedom begins with truth, but it cannot end there. It is not enough to diagnose correctly what makes a good life. We must be able to live it. We cannot be content with understanding what personal freedom might be. We must also be able to live into our freedom. We must be able to experience and enjoy a life that is good. We need grounded confidence that the life we long to live is, at least to a significant degree, within our grasp. We do not always see clearly how we can begin to live well. We often don't know how to take the first steps toward the virtues. Making any virtue a real part of our lives seems simply beyond our capacities. We want to experience personal freedom, but at times we are not optimistic about our chances. What we need is *hope*.

We often talk about hope as if it were mere wishful thinking. We see this understanding when we say, "I hope the Red Sox will win the series" or "I hope it won't rain tomorrow." Or, now that I live in Southern California, "I hope it *will* rain tomorrow." These are examples of wishful thinking, not hope. When I hope it won't rain tomorrow, I mean that I really want it not to rain, but I secretly think it will.

Philosopher Robert C. Roberts argues that emotions such as hope or joy are "concern-based construals."[2] A construal is how we see our concrete situation. It is a seeing *as*. A construal is not exactly a factual judgment. We feel fear, Roberts argues, when we see our situation *as* threatening regardless of whether that the threat is real. Even when a person who is afraid of snakes accurately judges that the snake he sees is not harmful, he may still cower in fear. His knowledge does not prevent him from seeing his situation as threatening. He feels fear, despite the fact that he *knows* there is nothing to be afraid of. Emotions are not simply a matter of how we see our situation, however. They are construals that are *concern based*. They involve things that matter to us. I do not feel fear just because it seems that something or

[2]Robert D. Roberts, *Spiritual Emotions: A Psychology of Christian Virtues* (Grand Rapids: Eerdmans, 2007), 11.

other is threatened. I feel fear only if something I care about appears to be threatened. If you tell me that the Detroit Pistons have little chance of making the playoffs, I won't feel fear or anxiety about it. I don't follow the NBA; I have no concern about their prospects.

If emotions in general are concern-based construals, what in particular is hope? Roberts explains: "Hope is a construal of one's future as holding good prospects."[3] A person has hope when she sees her future as good for her. An example might help. When I was halfway through my doctoral dissertation, I had one of many meetings with my adviser, Bill Alston. Since my topic involved philosophy of time, we talked a lot about past and future events. During this meeting, he casually used as an example, "So, in the future, when you complete your dissertation . . ." To be honest, I did not hear the rest of his sentence. I was overwhelmed that he said I would finish. He said it out loud! For the rest of the day, I had a bit of a bounce in my step. I came home and told Jeanie, "Alston thinks I will finish!" If *he* thinks I will finish, then *I* can believe I will finish! I had hope. I had a picture that the future I cared about would be good, not just in an abstract sense but good to me and good for me.

One difference between hope and wishful thinking is confidence. Real hope involves a confident vision of my future prospects as good. When I heard Alston say I would finish, I had confidence because he was a great philosopher. When I have hope, I am not *pretending* that my prospects are good. They *are* good, or I see them as good. Thus I face the future with an optimism that is grounded. Hope is tied to good reasons to think that the things I care most about will become a reality. If Roberts is on the right track, it is easy to see that personal freedom requires hope. I have to think that in the future, to a significant degree, I will live the life I want to live. I have to see that the things I care most about will go well.

---

[3]Ibid., 148.

Hope is largely future oriented, but it is a *present* construal about my future. My sense of my future shapes how I place myself in the present. It is in this way that my future affects my present. My present ability to navigate the world with confidence requires that I construe my future as good. Thus cultivating hope is not an escapist strategy to avoid the present. It is, rather, essential to navigating life now.

But *can* I be confident about my future? This kind of hope might seem too good to be true. It sounds naive. For our hope to be realistic, we must take seriously the significant challenges to construing our futures as good. There are two fundamental challenges to hope. First, it is simply hard to change. We often find ourselves in ruts. The task of managing our responsibilities each day can take all our attention and drain all our energy. The horizon of real change vanishes in the daily battle. Second, our optimism may get crushed by the experience of suffering. Every person experiences and witnesses significant suffering. Each of these challenges becomes more significant with the passage of time. We have to admit that the future does not always look bright.

I have always been a future-oriented person. I spent many hours daydreaming about becoming a philosopher, working in the university, and having a family. In my twenties and early thirties, the future was the realm of possibility. It seemed as if I could do everything I would want to do. My dreaming about the future helped me set long-term goals, many of which I have accomplished. A lot of my dreaming, however, turned out to be wishful thinking. I remember writing down a list of six languages I wanted to learn. It did not occur to me that I was doing nothing about any one of them. I was young, and the future was a long way off. Now, thirty years later, I have trouble finding my way through a simple Latin text. The passage of time is a special challenge for future-oriented people. With each decade, I have significantly less future ahead of me. Most of my life is past. When I hit the age of fifty, I began to cross things off my list. I came to grips with the fact that I will never learn New Testament Greek, let alone those other languages. I was no longer going to pretend that I would get to it eventually.

Our encounter with our own aging is multifaceted. This encounter is not limited to those who are looking at fifty in the rearview mirror. Even in our late twenties we can feel as though opportunities are being lost. With each choice we make, certain doors close, and opportunities become lost to us. We cannot take every path. Every path we choose leaves other paths unexplored. Our responsibilities increase, and we can long for days in the past that now seem carefree.

When we think about taking steps to become the kind of person we want to be, the passage of time is daunting. Even if we want to change, how do we begin? I mentioned earlier how our culture is infested with *moral atomism*. This is the notion that each of our choices is independent of any other choice. If I want to begin to live a certain way, I merely have to choose to do so. Reflecting on the difficulty of beginning to pursue any particular virtue, such as humility or generosity, reveals that we are marked deeply by the choices we have made. Moral atomism turns out to be an assumption prevalent among the young. Those of us who are well into (or through) our middle-aged years know better. Long-practiced habits of ordering our priorities and actions in particular ways have solidified the structure of our beliefs and loves. Our core identities are deeply ingrained in our being. Can we hope for real change?

Suffering brings another challenge to hope. Suffering challenges all of our cherished dreams about our lives. It can be like an invasion by an alien force. It rocks our stability and violates our expectations. As we age, suffering becomes more acute. We recognize that our own health will surely deteriorate. We see those around us increasingly struggling with disease. We can no longer see sickness merely as a temporary interruption. It is more likely to affect us for the rest of our lives. Suffering can make us wonder whether there is any good in our future at all. Optimism seems like wishful thinking. Can we have a confident assessment about out futures? It often seems not.

Hope lies at the center of the Christian story. This hope is not mere wishful thinking. It is a confident expectation that our future can and will be good, in spite of how difficult it is to change and the realities of suffering. We can capture this insight with the following observation: *In the Christian story, our story is never over.* We have hope when we welcome our future because it is good. In the Christian story our future *is* good.

I will explore two features of the Christian picture of the future. First, the Christian story offers secure hope of personal transformation that can begin now. We *can* begin to change! Second, it provides the grounds for confidence in the face of both aging and suffering. In the Christian story, our story is never over because God's story is never over. God is at work now, and God continues to work in our futures. The Christian story includes God's participation in our personal transformation, and it includes the fact that God has an ultimate destiny for each of us. God is committed to bringing that destiny to fruition.

The Christian story tells us first that the task of becoming the people we should be is not one we face alone. It is a startling thought that the creator of the universe is involved in the development of our character. We participate or cooperate with God in this endeavor. The apostle Paul writes, "The fruit of the Spirit is love, joy, peace, patience, kindness, generosity, faithfulness, gentleness, and self-control" (Gal 5:22-23). In context, he is contrasting a life centered on the self with a life that is both centered on God and cooperating with God's project of personal transformation. The character qualities he lists capture the kinds of virtues we think make for good relationships and an excellent life. He states that these are the "fruit of the Spirit." The metaphor of fruit is used often in the New Testament. Just as the fruit of a tree is a natural result of the healthy life of the tree, these qualities are the natural result of a life that allows the Spirit of God to work in us. God produces these qualities in us. This dynamic of cooperation is part of our dependent relation on God. We participate as we draw on God's strength and take small steps to order our loves around the divine character.

The notion that our story is never over reminds us that it is not too late to begin significant change. God continues to help us choose to think and act according to a new order of loves. That we have habits of behavior that are deeply entrenched does not make our habits permanent. To be sure, it requires some diligence to act consistently with the virtues we know to be significant. We can take the first steps and begin to experience a life characterized by the fruit God produces.

We discussed how, in the Christian story, human nature reflects God's nature. We were created, in part, to embody and display the kind of character qualities that reflect God's own nature. The fruit that Paul presents is a good snapshot of these. If God's purposes for us include that we experience and live according to these virtues, it makes sense that God will be active in helping us successfully live this kind of excellent life. Thus it is a vital part of the Christian story that God is with us in the project of navigating the world well.

Not only is God involved in our personal transformation now, but also the Christian story promises that God will complete the process of helping us become the people we want to be. The apostle John writes, "Beloved, we are God's children now; what we will be has not yet been revealed. What we do know is this: when he is revealed, we will be like him, for we will see him as he is" (1 Jn 3:2). When we see Jesus, we will be like him. This promise, reiterated throughout the New Testament, is that we will experience the character qualities that reflect God. In fact God uses all of the difficulties in our lives to help us reflect the virtues that mark the divine nature.

This process will not be completed in this life, but it will be completed. We see it partially finished in this life, but we will see it fully in the next. Theologian Francis Schaeffer talks of the promise of substantial healing in this life and complete healing in the next.[4] The personal transformation we undergo in this life is the first fruit or the indication of what is to come.

In addition to the hope of real change, the Christian vision of life gives us the resources to face aging and suffering. The inevitable suffering we experience does not have to defeat our hopes. The resources of the Christian story regarding our suffering involve three themes. First, God's plan of redemption is a plan of restored wholeness. This theme is grounded on the fact that our story is not over. Second, our suffering even now is not meaningless. It fits into God's plan to cultivate character and to bring us to wholeness. Third, the key to facing suffering is God's real presence with us. The suffering I face, as difficult as it may be, is a temporary challenge. My destiny is one of wholeness and flourishing. God is present with me to help me bear my sufferings well. Each of these themes is worth exploring.

That God's plan is for restored wholeness means that suffering and death do not get the last word. Paul writes that in the mission of Jesus, "The last enemy to be destroyed is death" (1 Cor 15:26). If death has been conquered, then my *life* does not end when this *body* dies. Jesus' own resurrection overcame death and paved the way for our life eternal. Jesus' resurrection plays this role in part because of the atoning nature of his death. His death was the final sacrifice for sin. Thus forgiveness, redemption, and restoration can be a reality for each person. We need only to respond to Jesus in trust and dependence. Two images in John's Revelation point to this restored wholeness.

> And I heard a loud voice from the throne saying,
> "See, the home of God is among mortals.
> He will dwell with them;
> they will be his peoples,

[4] Francis Schaeffer, *True Spirituality*, in *The Complete Works of Francis Schaeffer*, vol. 3, *A Christian View of Spirituality* (Westchester, IL: Crossway, 1982).

> and God himself will be with them;
> he will wipe every tear from their eyes.
> Death will be no more;
> mourning and crying and pain will be no more,
> for the first things have passed away."
>
> And the one who was seated on the throne said, "See, I am making all things new." Also he said, "Write this, for these words are trustworthy and true." (Rev 21:3-5)
>
> Then the angel showed me the river of the water of life, bright as crystal, flowing from the throne of God and of the Lamb through the middle of the street of the city. On either side of the river is the tree of life with its twelve kinds of fruit, producing its fruit each month; and the leaves of the tree are for the healing of the nations. (Rev 22:1-2)

These images speak of deep restoration. Tears will be wiped away, mourning and death will be gone, pain will be no more. There will be provision for the healing of the nations. All of the suffering will be healed, and lives will be restored. Human beings will live free in communion with one another and with God.

The second theme is that our suffering can be meaningful here and now. Making sense of our lives in the middle of our suffering *now* requires more than a good future. Our present must link with that future. Throughout the Christian story, we are reminded that it is through our response to suffering that we become the people we are meant to be—the people we want to be. To find meaning in our present suffering we must humbly accept this goal for our lives. It requires submitting to God's agenda of character re-formation. It is to cooperate with God's Spirit as we navigate our lives by the marks of the Spirit. We seek to respond with love, joy, peace, endurance, character, and hope. We do this by trusting God to give us the sight to recognize how we should respond and to give us the power to do so. Our lives continue to make sense to us because we relate our suffering to the very goal God has for us. The apostle James writes, "My brothers and sisters, whenever you face trials of any kind, consider it nothing but joy, because you know that the testing of your faith produces endurance; and let endurance have its full effect, so that you may be mature and complete, lacking in nothing" (Jas 1:2-4).

The third theme is that the defeat of evil, especially horrible evil, requires nothing less than the presence of God in this life and the next. Philosopher Eleonore Stump comments, "The beloved's closeness to God and her flourishing as the best person she can be will, therefore, be co-variant."[5] The great good for human beings, the good that characterizes human flourishing, comes with closeness to God. This closeness is often described as a union with God. The Christian vision of life insists that this union is possible to a significant degree in this life.

Union with God, in Christian thinking, is not a dissolving of the self. Union is not the absorption and dissolution of the human being into the substance of God. On the contrary, the human person is never more herself as when she is closest to God. The presence of God is a personal presence. It is an intimacy of relationship between two ontologically distinct persons. It is an intimacy that is closer than relationships between two human beings. God knows each human being perfectly. God also loves without measure. To be known and yet to be loved is the foundation of intimacy. In the Revelation of John, it is promised that those who overcome will be given a white stone, "and on the white stone is written a new name that no one knows except the one who receives it" (Rev 2:17). God gives a new name to each person in the life to come. On it is that person's own true name, the name known by her alone and by God.

[5]Eleonore Stump, *Wandering in Darkness: Narrative and the Problem of Suffering* (Oxford: Oxford University Press, 2010), 93.

The presence of God does more than comfort us in our sorrow. His presence heals, strengthens, and restores our broken humanity. We see this principle at work over and over in the earthly ministry of Jesus. There is a story told in three of the Gospels about a leper coming before Jesus (Mt 8:1-4; Mk 1:40-45; Lk 5:12-15). In the culture of Jesus' day, a leper was unclean. He could not take part in the religious life of the community. Nor should he mix with others in public. People were prohibited even from touching someone who was unclean. This man, cut off from his own society, breaks these norms to fall before Jesus. He states, "If you choose, you can make me clean." He is unsure. Would Jesus choose to help someone who was unclean? All three accounts indicate that (in the words of Mark) "Jesus stretched out his hand and touched him, and said to him, 'I do choose. Be made clean!'" (Mk 1:41). Jesus healed the leper. The important part is that Jesus did not heal the leper first and then touch him. He touched him first. He touched him while he was still untouchable. This is a story of more than physical healing. Jesus restores the core identity of the former outcast. He does so publicly. The man went away healed. More than that, his humanity was restored. In God's eyes, no one is unclean. The touch of God restores our broken humanity.

Aging and suffering do not conquer our grounds for hope. We can have a confident expectation that our futures are good. This confidence brings peace. Hope brings peace in that I can welcome my future. I do not regard it with anxiety. If I accept my future gladly, I am not at the mercy of my suffering. My peace is grounded in the confidence that I can keep my equilibrium no matter what happens. I can weather the storms without losing perspective. I can continue to navigate my life with a view to being the best person I can be.

Hope in my life involves construing my future as good for me. To the degree that I can trust that God is at work helping me become who I want to become, I see my future as hopeful. This hope carries me despite aging and suffering. Grasping the reality of the next life helps me navigate my aging. My story is not nearing its end. One chapter is approaching its close, but the story goes on. In atheistic stories each human being is ultimately defeated by suffering and death. Despite the contribution we may make to those around us, most of us will be forgotten in four generations. In the Christian story, suffering and death are defeated. Our story is never over.

I realize that the notion of eternal life sounds unbelievable to many people. It is central to the Christian story, however. After we die, our story continues. Many people think this part of the Christian story is irrelevant escapism, but it plays a central role. In fact, Immanuel Kant thought it was essential to moral thinking as a whole. Central to his ethical theory is the notion that virtue and happiness must coincide.[6] The morally good person must, he thought, experience flourishing. If our horizon is limited to this life, there can be no guarantee that a person of virtue will experience peace or contentment. Only if God continues the moral and spiritual work in a person's life after death can this connection between virtue and happiness be guaranteed. In the Christian story, our story is never over.

Many people find the Christian prospects of life after death unappealing. There are two related misconceptions of the Christian vision of eternal life that contribute to this resistance. First, the Christian picture of heaven is often linked with clouds and harps. It is thought to involve a sort of disembodied existence. Second, people think that eternal life will be something static. The association with clouds and harps comes from a combination of certain biblical imagery with popular images such as Looney Tunes cartoons. In the last book of the New Testament, there are a few images of the inhabitants of heaven playing golden harps. These are far from the only metaphors at work, however. Rather than a disembodied life in the clouds, the afterlife is described as being lived out by people who have been raised from the

---

[6]See, for example, Immanuel Kant, *A Critique of Pure Reason*, A812/B840; and *Religion Within the Boundaries of Mere Reason*, 6.6-6.7.

dead with bodies. The Christian story is not one of some semihuman soulish stuff surviving death. It is one in which the full human being—body, mind, and soul—is raised to new life forever. It is not in the clouds that eternal life happens. It begins now, in this life. The closing chapters of the New Testament describe a new *earth* with its central locale as a new *city*. Thus there will be culture, commerce, work, and art; in short, there will be all of the things that make human life rich and rewarding.

These fuller biblical images suggest that the picture of life after death is far from static. If, as is the case, the Christian story of eternal life is dynamic, there will be growth and challenges anew. The best analogy I can think of is that of a rich marriage. Jeanie and I have been married since 1985. That is a pretty long time to live with the same person. Is it boring? Not at all! Our relationship is dynamic. It grows. There is a rich combination of the comfort of long-established patterns of relating to each other and the ever-new discoveries that come from mutual enjoyment. A good marriage over many years is the opposite of boring.

We can show the plausibility of the Christian view of eternal life by pointing out how it fits with the entire Christian story. If God created us with a distinctly human nature that grounds the value of our human enterprises of knowledge, beauty, relationships, and work, it makes sense that these features will be an essential part of our life with God. It would be strange if life after death included a bare shell of what makes us human beings now. The Christian story grounds our longings and our hopes that everything human will be preserved and redeemed.

Epilogue

HUMAN ASPIRATION AND THE CHRISTIAN STORY

The fundamental assumption of this book is that each human being has the same task. This task is to navigate the world the best we can. We each aim to do and be what seems good to us to do and to be. We also aim to avoid doing and being those things that seem bad or less fruitful. We navigate the world based on the things that seem true or are most important. Our desires and commitments, together with our beliefs, provide the framework for our life task. With this assumption in mind, I set out to make the case that the Christian story grounds and explains the things we care about most. The central features of the Christian story involve God, who creates the world and makes us in the divine image. We have meaning and value that is objective and cosmic, rather than being simply subjective and local. God made a good and beautiful world for us to explore and cultivate. Despite the fact that the world has been twisted by our insisting on our independence from God, it is still a good and beautiful place. God's purposes for us outlive this life and include the healing of the effects of evil. Justice will surely come.

The deeper concerns we share involve our commitment to people, our love of goodness and beauty, and our quest for freedom. All of these things fit within the Christian story. That our deepest concerns involve persons connects with the idea that in the Christian story the most fundamental reality is personal. That God is good explains why goodness is primary and why goodness is good for us. God as Master Artist gives meaning to our creative endeavors. Our personal freedom is secured in the Christian story because our story is never over.

I have tried to make it clear that the Christian story far exceeds the atheistic story in its resources to capture our longings. I did not aim to argue philosophically or deductively for my claim. Instead, I tried to show it through unwrapping the features of our deeper concerns and by explaining the elements of the Christian story that connect to those features. If the reader recognizes her own commitments in my exposition of human longings, she might be persuaded of the efficacy of the Christian story to explain them. If she does not recognize herself in my discussion, she may not change her mind about what the Christian story has to offer in this regard.

I also did not argue or try to argue that the Christian story is true. As I said, I do think it is true, but I think the question of its truth is not interesting to most people. It might be the case that the Christian story is false, even if it does ground and explain what we care about better than alternative stories. I think that a strong case can be made for the truth of Christianity. To argue that the Christian story is true or likely to be true, however, is outside the scope of this book. There are many others that contribute well to that task.

Perhaps I may recommend some next steps for the reader. If you are somewhat persuaded of the case I put forward, the next stop for you will be to think about whether the Christian story is true. How would one go about that task? I can recommend some things to read that might get you going in the right discussion.[1] But what if you are not persuaded that the Christian story grounds and explains our deepest concerns? In this case, I think it might be fruitful for you to identify exactly what failed to persuade you. What parts of my case seemed the weakest to you? Were any of them strong? Thinking through the strengths and weaknesses of someone's case helps us engage it well. I would be lying if I did not admit that I would like you to think through my discussion again. Perhaps on a second look you will see things a little differently. I would also encourage you to identify the things that you believe *are* your deepest concerns. Recognizing those things might enable you to see the resonance between your concerns and the argument I have put forward.

A third class of readers involves those who already hold to the Christian story. If you are one of these readers, you were probably not waiting to see whether I could persuade you of my main claims. The next step for you might be to continue to explore the way that Christianity makes sense of what people care about most. This exploration may help you see at a deeper personal level what it means to be a follower of Jesus. In addition, your reflection may help you answer other people's questions in a way that makes sense to them.

My hope is that whichever reader you are, you will see yourself in my musings. As a result, I do hope you will feel and think differently

---

[1]Two of my books might be helpful: *Thinking About God: First Steps in Philosophy* (Downers Grove, IL: InterVarsity Press, 2004) and *A Reasonable God: Engaging the New Face of Atheism* (Waco, TX: Baylor University Press, 2009). The first is a very basic introduction. The second interacts with the arguments for atheism in the works of Richard Dawkins, Daniel Dennett, Sam Harris, and Christopher Hitchens. Another very clear work is Tim Keller, *The Reason for God* (New York: Dutton, 2008). A comprehensive and well-written historical defense of the resurrection of Jesus is Michael R. Licona's *The Resurrection of Jesus: A New Historiographical Approach* (Downers Grove, IL: InterVarsity Press, 2010).

about what the Christian story is and why it is important to the things that matter. I am convinced that thinking well about these things is critical to a life that is rich. Such reflection will help us be closer to what is true, what is good, and what is beautiful. It helps us become the people we want to become.

General Index

Scripture Index

Old Testament

New Testament